THE OFFICIAL GUIDE TO

DISCO

DANCE

STEPS

THE
OFFICIAL GUIDE
TO

DISCO
DANCE
STEPS

by Jack Villari and
Kathleen Sims Villari

CHARTWELL BOOKS INC.

COVER AND CHAPTER LEAD-IN DESIGN **joe mistak**

ILLUSTRATIONS AND BOOK DESIGN **kent starr**

ORIGINAL PHOTOGRAPHY **patrick snook**

EDITORIAL DIRECTOR **jim hargrove**

The Official Guide to Disco Dance Steps
Copyright © 1978 Jack Villari and Kathleen Sims Villari
Published by Chartwell Books Inc.
A Division of Book Sales Inc.
110 Enterprise Avenue
Secaucus, New Jersey 07094

1   2   3   4   5   6   7   8   9   10

Manufactured in the United States of America

*To Mom and Dad for the wisdom of parenthood
and Maria and Brian for the optimism of youth*

Library of Congress Cataloging in Publication Data

Villari, Jack,
      The official guide to disco dance steps.

      Includes index.
      1. Disco Dancing.   2. Discotheques.   I. Villari,
Kathleen Sims,   joint author   II. Title.
III. Title: Disco dance steps.
GV1796.D57V54   793.3   78-9849
0-89009-259-1

CONTENTS

PREFACE

The Official Guide To Disco Dance Steps is the culmination of a four-year research study and is the direct response to a loud cry for an official guide to disco dance instruction. Being involved in show business and media communications all our lives, we were totally aware of the coming disco phenomenon long before its emergence into the world of John Q. Public. It's all really basic when you analyze it.

Throughout history man has developed a repeated pattern of expressing himself through dance, becoming a spectator when it became too complex and participating again when it identified with the masses. With a keen ear to the musical trends, any astute musician could pretty well have predicted the advent of disco fever. The result: the beginning of a new participation era and the Golden Age of Dance.

To arrive at this totally unique approach to dance, we combined information from private collections of dance literature with individual pupil-teacher experiences and interviews from professional dancers, disco operators, DJs, and recording companies. Judging disco dance contests throughout the country, we couldn't help but realize the one recurring fact—that it was the style and fluidity of movement that singled out the eye-catching dancer.

We've heard it said repeatedly: "Disco dancing looks like so much fun, I'd love to be able to get out there and dance. Do you give private lessons?" Well, don't let this shock you, but for most people, private lessons aren't necessary. At our American Dance Center school in south suburban Chicago, we have trained thousands of nondancers in group classes, and to the point where they could get out on the floor and execute show-stopping routines. As a matter of fact, many of our students now are giving exhibition demonstrations, winning cash prizes in weekly dance contests and even teaching disco in their own areas. Some have become professional dancers and are now experiencing the glamor and bright lights of show business.

We have developed this disco dance handbook to guide you step by step just as we do in our classes. This easy-to-follow guide will help you develop an individualized dance style and the self-confidence that will put *you* in the spotlight. Notice that even in the more complex dances, there is very little need for confusing footstep diagrams to follow. This is because our main philosophy is to develop *first* a basic vocabulary of steps and movement patterns. Once you've mastered these, you will be well on your way to any disco dance. You might even want to make it a family affair. Everyone from junior to grandma will find it hard to resist the rhythms and movement of disco.

INTRODUCTION

DISCOVER YOURSELF THROUGH DISCO

Discomania is a phenomenon, a power, a statement of today. Discomania is an irresistibly danceable beat, a catchy new style of music, an exhilarating form of entertainment and an all-encompassing cultural force that has taken America and the world by storm.

Disco dancing and all its trimmings are no longer the exclusive domain of an avant garde few. Estimates point to a disco audience numbering from 40 to 50 million persons, including folks of ages 13 to 60, representatives of all walks of life and members of every racial and ethnic group found in the world. And the number of discotheques in the U.S. and Europe increases every month. The U.S. had at least 15,000 clubs during 1977, despite the high failure rate of new discos and those deserted by a demanding and fickle public.

Discomania has gone the way of the 20th century's most compelling social trends, involving every facet of the communications media and far-flung business markets. In the U.S., discomania is a product as well as a sales tool. Businessmen from coast to coast jump at the chance to get in on the disco boom, by investing in clubs, films, records, sound products, lighting and special effects, consulting and design firms, disco record pools for DJs, disco franchises, dance schools, disco clothing and many other areas.

This enthusiasm has been matched and surpassed by the public, which swarms the dance floors in numbers unequaled since the big-band era. Everyone wants to disco, and the business world has responded with inimitable speed in serving every disco-oriented whim of the dancers. Disco fans can play pinball, pool or backgammon, meet others and engage in lively conversation, watch old Marx Brothers films, drink cocktails or soda pop, dine on sumptuous spreads or munch on popcorn, dance or watch, see or be seen in the variety of today's clubs. Exclusive clubs that admit no one under age 25 are widespread, and for the younger discomaniacs who can't get into Studio 54 and similar spots, there is even roller disco, in which the dancers can do extra-quick turns possible only on roller skates. And, of course, promoters and owners have made sure that no matter where you might be, there is a disco right around the corner—in the chain hotels and health spas, in department store basements and restaurants, at airports and in resort locales. Franchises like 2001 and Tramps have been augmented by easily recognizable disco chains such as the Club 747 of America, a string of discos which was born in Buffalo, New York, and features discos housed in old Boeing 747 airplanes outfitted with airline seats and stewardess-waitresses and hostesses. And, if you seek the ultimate in convenience and exclusivity, there are disco services that will bring all the fixings for a disco party right into your living room.

The disco scene has become BIG business throughout the world, and as the profits keep rolling in, new disco jobs and products are created and promotion is stepped up to a true fever pitch. Big business means big money for some. Paramount's film *Saturday Night Fever* and Columbia's *Thank God It's Friday* have been instant successes. In Variety's list of the top 50 grossing films, *Saturday Night Fever* had grossed $32,328,642 after only 26 weeks on the chart; after only four weeks on the list, *Thank God It's Friday* had brought in

$4,219,881. Compare those figures to the $29 million that the Academy Award winning film *Rocky* made in a full 45 weeks, and you can begin to visualize the potency of discomania.

Disco also has gained worldwide recognition as a social force. *Billboard's* famous Disco Forum, which held its fourth annual event during 1978, was made a semiannual event during that year by popular demand. Also in 1978, New York City declared the first national disco week, surrounding the dates of Disco Forum IV in June. In London, British newspapers and various recording labels combined forces to sponsor the first World Disco Dance Championship during the summer of 1978. The sponsors expected 39 countries to be represented at the huge contest, and planned to award $25,000 worth of prizes. Another major event is the Discom Expo, to be held in Deauville, France, during the summer of 1979. Sponsored by French disco promotion companies and a top French disco magazine, the convention will be focused on marketing and merchandising of disco music and hardware. If as successful as predicted, the expo will be an annual event.

In the midst of all this excitement is the lone dancer or would-be dancer who often doesn't know quite what to expect from the disco scene. Hence, this book. *The Official Guide to Disco Dance Steps* can be your disco dancer's bible. Through an insider's view of the disco scene, and easy-to-follow dance instructions, you can develop a whole new self-image and an individual dance style that will create memorable moments for you as it has for millions of others. The information in the following chapters will acquaint you with the rhythm and excitement of the disco world and, hopefully, will encourage you to broaden your dance skills and discover yourself through the excitement that surrounds the disco generation.

One of the most fascinating qualities of discomania, however, is the fact that the disco generation includes people of all ages and all levels of movement skill. Anyone can learn to do the dances in this book! Whether you are in the public eye or on the private scene, if you're a dancer or just want to move like one, this book is for you. We've written this handbook so that it can be used easily by the casual, social dancer as well as the actor or actress and anyone else in the performing or modeling fields whose future career potential depends on a basic knowledge of disco dance. With the importance of disco in all these fields, quite a large number of individuals are included.

The crucial factor in the adaptability of our instructions is that, basically, we all start out with the same tools—a mind that can think disco, a body that can move in an amazing number of ways, and a desire to move in an enjoyable fashion to irresistible musical accompaniment. Herein lies Secret Number One: With regular repetition, anyone can develop the mind and body coordination necessary to dance. Professional dancers spend hours each day exercising their bodies so that they can achieve certain movements and movement patterns at will. So don't expect to read this book once and head for the dance floor without any preliminary practice. In fact, there is one important rule of thumb used by dancers that should be kept in mind throughout the learning process: Discipline must always come before freedom. In other words you must train each and every part of your body to move until the movements become automatic, *before* you can enjoy the freedom of developing your own style, quality of movement, or disco look.

Frequent exercise will allow you more freedom of expression and stylized movement. Whether you are a three-times-a-week dancer, or you just go out three times a year, it is wise to prepare your body by working through the basic dance exercises given here. Those who do dance frequently will notice a marked improvement in their abilities to improvise and to develop nuances in the basic patterns. An additional benefit of regular dancing is reduced fatigue, increased energy, quicker movement and gradual elimination of morning-after aches and pains. It stands to reason that you can't expect to dance your best on a moment's notice if you haven't prepared yourself one step at a time. The body is similar to any other complex machine; it can perform many functions, but works best when it is well maintained.

The step-by-step approach is the basic philosophy behind this book. Using professional secrets and a proven learning system, we present easy-to-follow instructions that take you all the way from the most basic dance movements through the flourishes and accents the accomplished dancer can build on. **Even if you already consider yourself a dancer, don't try to skip the early sections in order to go directly to the dance instruction in Chapter 5. To follow any step in our system, you must know the material that precedes it.** In addition, our initial exercise routine can be beneficial to even the most advanced dancer, by relaxing and toning up muscles and relieving tension, besides improving your basic movement quality.

Chapter 1 will introduce you to the world of dancing in general, and disco in particular, through a brief look at the art of dance through the ages. Once you realize that dance is older than history and the most natural of man's abilities, you will begin to feel more confident in your own ability to move. Chapter 2 is a general discussion of the disco sound, that driving beat that uses sophisticated technology and complex arrangements to drive a floor full of disco fans into a frenzy of dance. Get to know the sound of today; once the disco rhythm is in your blood, you're a discomaniac for good.

Chapters 3 through 5 form the core of your dancer's bible. Step by step, the text, illustrations and photos tell you *exactly* how to achieve the disco look. Not only will you learn the latest disco dances, you also will be ready to develop a personal style that no one else can claim as their own. Follow the instructions in those chapters at your own pace. Don't be afraid to return to an earlier section if you're in doubt about how to execute a particular step, but do try to master each part before moving on to the next. In the long run, you'll progress more quickly.

The final chapter in the book gives you an inside look at the trappings of the disco world—who's into it, where, how, why and when. Armed with newfound dance skills and a mind and body tuned in to the disco wavelength, you'll be able to hold your own on any dance floor. So, turn the pages and discover yourself through disco—you'll be glad you did.

1
DISCOMANIA:
A
History
of the
Phenomenon

Few subjects have received as much publicity in recent years as the phenomenon of discomania. Through newspaper and magazine articles, films, television and radio broadcasts, we have been inundated with various views of the disco scene. Full-page photos depict the antics of glamor-seekers at New York's Studio 54, and gossip columnists tell us which celebrities were seen dancing until dawn at which well-known clubs. Mention the word disco to an arm-chair spectator, and you immediately call up visions of a fantasy world filled exclusively with the beautiful people.

But strip today's discotheque of its elaborate trappings, and the remaining picture is one seen again and again through history: men and women engaging in dance for celebration, for recreation, for expression. What makes today's disco different from the Charleston of the '20s or the jitterbug of the '40s is, of course, that it *is* a child of our modern age. There is no mistaking the flashing colors, intricate dance floors and swirling fashions of disco. The 1970s and beyond are stamped in every beat of the music, every blink of the light shows, every stitch of the dancers' attire. Disco is in the news because it *does* have something new to offer.

That certain something that keeps disco in the forefront, however, is hardly unique to our decade. Whether they consider the disco scene avant garde or nostalgic, whether they want to see or to be seen, most enthusiasts are drawn to the discotheques by the main attraction—the dance floor. If you're a long time stranger to the dance floor, you may find it difficult to imagine the irresistible magnetism of moving to a rhythmic beat, or of stepping in harmony with a partner. Don't rush off and exchange your dancing shoes for a pair of sensible oxfords. The simple dance exercise routine in Chapter 3 will help you master the basics of dancing.

To complete your understanding of today's disco world, read on. The following brief history traces the development of dance through the ages, illustrating the steps and styles that arose from various cultures and times, and now play a part in disco dancing.

Many of the movements seen on today's dance floors originated centuries ago, from peoples as disparate as the royalty of the French Renaissance to the tribes of North

American Indians. But the most important point to remember when you walk out onto that dance floor is that you're carrying on a lot more than family or ethnic tradition.

As long as man has walked the earth, he has danced as well. Dance is the oldest of man's arts; older than language or music. Early man often used dance and movements in place of language to express his thoughts. Some of these gestures are still in evidence, as people throughout most of the world nod their heads to indicate "yes," shake their heads from side to side to say "no," and even raise their shoulders with an outward gesture of the hands to signify "I don't know." Over the centuries, peoples of various regions and nations developed their own particular gestures, just as dialects and colloquialisms evolved in their languages.

Through the ages, there has always been one common denominator—rhythm. Rhythm has always evoked movement, and dance is simply a rhythmic movement of the body. It is no wonder that dance has flourished since the beginning of time, for rhythm is all around us. Time and again, science has shown us that where there is rhythm, there is dance. We are continually discovering new forms of dance used by animals and insects to communicate thoughts and messages to their own kind.

Even the language-oriented human species shows us on many levels that dance is natural to inhabitants of our earth. Observe any child: free of the inhibitions that plague adults, children move freely and joyfully, always expressing their thoughts and feelings through exuberant movements. To further prove that rhythm and dancing are natural to us, try watching alleged nondancers clap their hands or tap their feet unconsciously when they hear a rhythmic beat.

Perhaps it was inevitable that dance should come to the fore during our time. After decades of automation and technological progress stifled our physical abilities, the world turned once again to the subtleties of expression without words. Just about everyone jogs or practices yoga, and volumes have been published on such subjects as "body language."

We often think of this trend—and the disco phenomenon—as something born entirely of our modern times. Actually, our civilization has merely come full circle, returning to an instinct basic to all mankind. Like everything else, dance history repeats itself, and disco can be understood as part of a general pattern in the development of dance.

The Early Years

Dance actually originated before recorded history. Prehistoric paintings indicate that the primitive cave dwellers of our species engaged in some form of dance. Whether they danced for expression, celebration or ritual is not known, but some of the painted figures suggest the same movements we see on today's dance floors. For those who think that disco is too progressive for their tastes, compare photos of ancient cave paintings with today's dancers.

It all began with the primitive tribal societies. To these people, dance was a common activity, and everyone participated. The dances and the rhythms were pure and simple but strong, as were the emotions expressed. These dancers brought us our first drum—a hollow log which was beaten with a stick to keep everyone moving together.

Primitive dances were mainly danced as rituals, and were frequent events. The tribal society danced to celebrate the harvest, to worship their gods, to bring rain or sunshine, to increase fertility or hasten healing—in short, to express their feelings and reactions to every part of human life. As in today's disco, these primitive dancers usually created a total atmosphere of involvement, using dramatic bursts of smoke and fire, body paint, elaborate costumes, and compelling rhythmic sounds to stimulate all the senses of the participants.

The men usually dominated the ceremonial dances, a fact we find repeated in later eras, as men come to the foreground during most peaks of dance participation. In theatrical dance of today, the rise of male stars accompanies the popularity that dance now enjoys. The prima ballerina and Ziegfeld Girls of the past have been replaced in the limelight by Edward Villela, Rudolf Nureyev, Mikhail Baryshnikov and others. And in the social dance world, the image of John Travolta from *Saturday Night Fever* has been enough to draw countless formerly reluctant men back to the dance floor.

As civilizations developed, dancing became a means of social enjoyment as well as ceremony. Individual cultures gradually developed national traditions and styles, just as they adopted a verbal language. In general, these early dances, which we call folk dances, were little more complex than the primitive dances, and were designed to include large groups of participants. Most were line or circle dances, which were embellished according to the society's development of music. Often, the steps were lively and exhilarating, providing yesterday's answer to tennis or jogging for the working man and woman.

Just like language, cuisine or clothing styles, dance began to reflect the lifestyles and cultural heritage of its creators. In most cases recorded by history, the evolution process began sluggishly. But in the civilization of ancient Greece, dance reached one of its earliest peaks. Along with their great intellectual advances, the Greeks mastered the physical skills and arts. In fact, they considered the physical and mental arts equally important. Socrates said that the best dancers made the best warriors, and that to become a ''philosopher king,'' one's physical skills must equal those of the mind.

Centuries after the ancient Greek civilization died, the peasants of other nations were performing simpler dances which survive today. Among them were the Russian cossack, the Italian tarantella, the Irish jig and the Spanish flamenco. There also was the Bavarian landler, a slow, turning dance for couples which eventually spawned the waltz. The Hungarian czardas was another, a national dance done to the music of gypsy fiddlers. And in the Far East, the bharata natya developed; an ancient temple dance, the oldest form of Indian dancing, performed by a single dancer.

The Art of the Elite— Courting and Escorting

During the Middle Ages, dance stagnated along with the other arts and sciences. Folk dances continued to evolve, but we have few records of significant changes in dance styles. The only event of note is again a reflection of the times. The era's feudal system gave every-thing to the rich—the land holders—and nothing to the lowly serfs. Eventually, dance, too, was restricted to the royal courts, where it floundered in obscurity.

Dance reached a second peak during the Renaissance period. Participation remained limited to the royal courts, but with a nudge from France's Louis XIV, members of the nobility developed dances that involved new and more complex steps.

During the 16th and 17th centuries, the court of the fabled Sun King flourished, overflowing with elegant ladies and gentlemen whose only goal in life was to gain favor at the court through their charming manners and rich costumes. Stately dance steps became an integral part of the regular parade, and as competition among the nobility spurred innovations in clothing and music, so did it force the creation of new dance steps. Many of these dances emphasized walking steps and gallantries, but they also required new physical skills. To develop those skills, members of the court devised a regimen of regular exercises to be used by dancers, as well as actors and athletes. The syllabus involved dedicated training that was not for everyone. This was actually the beginning of classical ballet, whereby dancers adhere to specific rules and movements in their practice and performance. But more importantly, it transformed dancing into an activity for the elite, in which the skilled became the entertainment for the rich.

Early dances from the Renaissance period included the graceful pavanne and saraband, which allowed royal participants to display their perfected manners. As dance increased in popularity, it spread to the peasant towns as well. Once in the mainstream of dance, the common man took the opportunity to add his own innovations. One such dance was the *Volta,* in which the men lifted their partners into the air, using their thigh as a seat. Compared to the other stately dances, the Volta was shockingly vulgar, and may have been the first of a long string of dances initially prohibited from polite society. The Volta, like its successors, eventually was accepted by the royal courts as well as the peasants.

The gavotte and the minuet were the most famous of the dances to emerge from this era. The gavotte was a lively step danced by peasants to music in 4/4 time. The minuet was sedate, and was danced by couples to 3/4 time; it has been called the forerunner of the waltz. Both dances remained popular for almost 150 years.

The Romantic Era— Development of Partner Dancing

The Renaissance years brought us partner dancing in the minuet. But it wasn't until the time of the French Revolution that dancing truly became an activity for couples. The Viennese waltz, which was also danced to 3/4 time, romanticized partner dancing. In an era when unrequited love and fainting ladies were *de rigeur,* the waltz was a fitting entry into the dance world. The 19th century was also the puritanical Victorian period, in which dancing was the only acceptable form of public physical contact between men and women. This couldn't help but increase the attraction of this dizzying dance in which the man's arms were entwined around his partner's waist.

Again, a dance arose in counterpoint to the waltz—the polka. Still popular in several nations today, the polka is a bouncy dance set to 2/4 time.

The 19th century was a time of change for most of the world, but social dance remained relatively static. The waltz and the polka continued to dominate the dance floors, and the rigid Victorian attitudes stifled the individuality and creativity shown by today's amateurs.

The American Way— The Ragtime Revolution

The first two decades of the 20th century brought a major revolution to the art of social dance. Along with flappers, Prohibition-born speak-easies, and the gorgeous Ziegfeld Girls, came the glorious silver screen. Soon came the heyday of the Hollywood musical, with its lavish dance productions and matinee idols. Millions of viewers suddenly were able to see the most famous stars dance across movie screens in their hometowns. The movies encouraged the glorification of the American dream girl, but even more importantly, they brought men back to the dance forefront. When Rudolf Valentino tangoed exotically across the screen between 1912 and 1920, women swooned—and men swore they would learn to dance. And dance they did, in Art Deco clubs from New York to the French Riviera.

The style of the tango was perfectly suited to the tastes of the day. Imported to Central America by African slaves during the early part of the 19th century, the dance then made its way to Argentina and Uruguay, where it picked up elements of the habanera and the bolero. In its present form, the dance was made popular—mainly by Valentino—around the time of World War I.

After World War I, the real revolution began with the introduction of jazz music. Americans tagged the 4/4 rhythms "ragtime" music. The beat was deeply rooted in the rhythms of the American Negro, and it inspired lively dance steps that shocked those still living in the Victorian era. However, ragtime hung on, and actually spawned two long-lived dances of the century—the fox trot and the quick step. These and other variations were suited to the small dance floors provided by the jazz hotspots. Those small floors, in turn, encouraged the development of more couple dances.

In the meantime, moviegoers dreamed of going to the glamorous nightclubs they saw on the silver screen. New York glamor spots like the Copacabana and the Latin Quarter were *the* places to go. And as the nightclub patrons began to catch on to the ragtime rhythm, new musicians, singers and clubs became the vogue. One famous spot, called the Cotton Club, was *the* place to go after the other clubs closed. There, the beautiful people of the 1920s and 1930s flocked to hear the new sounds of black performers such as Duke Ellington, Cab Calloway and to view the dance stylings of Bill "Bojangles" Robinson.

The movie industry, of course, picked up the ragtime theme, and new dances spread quickly across the country. The rebellion of the flapper era was reflected in dances like the Charleston, the Suzy Q, the shimmy and the black bottom. Hollywood pumped out flick after flick, each one glorifying the Charleston through elaborately choreographed scenes. The Charleston and its variations held sway through the 1920s, with additions of steps such as the Lindy Hop, a dance named in honor of Charles Lindbergh's solo flight of 1927, and the Big Apple, named after New York City, which had become the dance capital of the world.

Repeating the basic circumstances surrounding dance of the Renaissance period, steps grew in complexity and in the skill they required. And soon, many participants were taking to the sidelines to watch those with more skill. This trend led to the introduction of the dance contest.

By the beginning of the 1930s, Hollywood, Broadway and the numerous dance halls took the dance contest one step further. While Carmen Miranda dipped and swayed on the dance floors of films, John and Jane Doe endured grueling dance sessions for an entirely different reason. Entrepreneurs took advantage of the popularity of dance and the tragedy of the Great Depression and came up with the infamous dance marathon.

In these events, men and women desperate to earn enough money to support their families put themselves through the physical and emotional agony of non-stop dancing contests in the hope of winning monetary prizes. The onlookers paid to watch the drama unfold: To draw bigger audiences, contest operators often established painful endurance tests, or held special exhibitions by the contestants at the end of each day. To keep the contests going even longer, the audience often threw coins to the couples who performed the best.

In one marathon, the participants danced for 3,780 hours—22 weeks and 3½ days of dancing. The operators of the contest cut the 15-minute-per-hour rest period to three minutes during the last two weeks of the contest, and dropped the rest period entirely during the last 52½ hours. The prize? A mere $1,000—a lot of money for the time, but only about 26 cents per hour in wages.

Often, starlets and would-be starlets entered the dance marathons in hopes of attracting the attention of talent scouts who attended the contests. Dancing was such a strong element of the 1930s that the marathon became a breeding ground for new talent.

The Latin Connection

During the 1930s dance peak, ragtime rhythms moved over for a newcomer to the American dance scene—Latin music. A South American influence began to creep into the movements of the fox trot and the Charleston, a trend that also plays a great part in today's disco.

On Broadway and in Hollywood, dance continued to thrive, as Fred Astaire, Ginger Rogers, Ann Miller and others brought the latest styles to the smallest towns and the largest cities. Films also exposed the Latin styles to dancers, the first steps being the rumba and the paso doble. Originally from Cuba, the rumba is danced to music in 4/4 time, with lots of percussion instruments and rhythms of Spanish and Negro influence. Basically, the rumba was performed in one spot, requiring the dancers to sway their hips and keep their knees loose and relaxed.

The paso doble is danced to Spanish music, with bright, spicy rhythms, in march time. Every beat is accented in the dance, with the dancers doing one step at a time to each beat.

The Brazilian samba, introduced at the 1930s World's Fair, was the mainstem for dance variations during the decade. Originally a folk dance, it became a popular ballroom dance for couples done to 2/4 time.

The conga was a dance imported from the French Riviera, in which the dancers formed a long line with hands on each other's hips and weaved in and out of the liveliest night spots. Later, the mambo was introduced. Similar to the rumba and done to music in 4/4 time, the mambo is a syncopated step of Cuban origin. Mambo music featured distinctive drums and gourds in the percussion sections.

In turn, the mambo was followed by the merengue, a simpler version of the samba and rumba variations. The merengue came from the West Indies and featured a rumba hip motion and lame-duck styling in which the steps were taken with a limp.

The Swing Era

As technology continued to bring us new

forms of entertainment, dance became a focal point of recreation in America and in Europe. Juke boxes, radio dance broadcasts and Broadway revues supplemented the lavish treatment dance received in films. And the blossoming recording industry brought the glamor of music and dancing right into the living rooms of the American public.

During the late 1930s, Glenn Miller and the other musicians of the pre-war years discovered the sound that would create a whole new dance age. The big bands arrived, and Americans danced to the tunes of bands led by Guy Lombardo, Tommy and Jimmy Dorsey, Harry James, Benny Goodman and Paul Whiteman. Other names that will bring back fond memories for some music lovers include Lawrence Welk, Kay Kaiser, Stan Kenton, Chuck Foster, Woody Herman, Dizzy Gillespie, Count Basie and scores of others. The beat of the decade was lively but smooth, and Americans called it "swing." Again, ballrooms sprouted up to accommodate the big bands and the big crowds they drew on their worldwide tours. The new sound usually featured horn or drum solo sections and big ensemble arrangements. The immediate popularity of swing music and bands created a soaring record market and a widely diverse dance style. Some dancers watched, while others distinguished themselves from the ballroom crowds with fancy footwork and intricate partner styling. Once again, trophies and prizes were awarded in dance contests held for outstanding couples.

Unfortunately, World War II interrupted the swing era, and put a damper on the social dance world. Most of the men were at war, so dance was left to the teenagers and the women who stayed at home, listening to swing records and dancing alone. The World War II dance hall was the living room.

The jitterbug that lasted for about 20 years—with alterations, of course—actually was born during World War II. Started by GIs dancing at USOs and other halls, the jitterbug involved lots of gymnastic movements, some of which were considered tabu on polite dance floors. The jitterbug, like its predecessors, survived the war through popular demand. But the exertion it required from dancers relegated it to the sock hops and proms of teenagers, and World War II took its toll on adult dancing.

The war-time conditions created a new wave in music. With their loved ones away at war, Americans turned to music with romantic and emotional lyrics. Fewer couples were available for dancing, so the radio stations and recording companies turned to music that stressed singers and lyrics rather than rhythm. Post-war dancers swayed gently to the melodies of crooners Frank Sinatra and Bing Crosby, plus singers like Ella Fitzgerald, Perry Como and many others.

The Rock and Roll Phenomenon

The early 1950s brought television into the American home, and this medium, like radio, films and juke boxes, spread the dancing fever. The 1950s brought prosperity and optimism to the U.S., and along with them came livelier music. Dancers began to revive the challenge and pleasure of doing the exciting Latin dances that had been the pre-war rage. Arthur and Kathryn Murray opened their famous dance studios across America. By the time the Murrays were giving Americans private lessons in their living rooms through television, dancers were beginning to master the Latin dances, and to beg for more. The answer to their pleas was the cha-cha, a dance which has been molded to the 1970s and can be seen on disco dance floors. The cha-cha was all the rage during the early '50s. With help from the recording industry, cha-cha songs were heard everywhere, and everyone learned to dance.

The less challenging, but quite popular, entries into dance history from the 1950s included the bunny hop and the hokey pokey, both intended for large groups of participants. With its weaving line pattern of jumps and kicks the bunny hop was the 1950s answer to the conga line.

The greatest change in dance of the decade—perhaps in dance of the century—came with the introduction of rock and roll music. Actually, rock and roll was just the beginning of a current dance renaissance; dance has undergone more changes and progress between the 1950s and the 1970s than during the last two centuries.

Rock and roll, a phrase coined by New York disc jockey Alan Freed, was characterized by pounding rhythms and raucous lyrics, much to the dismay of adult onlookers. Rock and roll has its roots in the music of Fats Domino and his self-proclaimed successor, Chubby Checker, who introduced the twist. An uninhibited dance in which the torso and hips were twisted in counterpoint, the twist was considered a daring innovation of self-expression. There was no required footwork, no pattern that had to be followed. This dance was the forerunner of the dances of the 1960s and of today's disco steps.

During the same wild era, Elvis Presley earned a reputation as the king of rock and roll, as he produced record after hit record for American teenagers. Presley had—and still has—millions of faithful fans around the world, and it all began with an appearance by Elvis on the Ed Sullivan Show, a well known television variety program. Millions watched Elvis on the television screen—from the waist up. The star's wild hip gyrations and uninhibited style convinced the network to film only the top half of his body.

Another television contribution during the 1950s and 1960s was Dick Clark's American Bandstand, in which teenagers danced for the television camera, and listened to newly released rock and roll tunes. Meanwhile, Hollywood jumped on the bandwagon by cranking out movies in which Frankie Avalon and Annette Funicello boogied at beach parties. And on the stage, Broadway shows like "Bye-Bye Birdie" and "West Side Story" borrowed from the rock and roll and Latin dances to gain new vitality. Mellow was out—rock was in.

Rock and roll became a multi-faceted phenomenon. A new style of vocalization and the revival of a rhythmic beat were established by young people of the 1950s. For the first time, the teenagers were setting the musical and dance trends, and the record industry began to look to the youth for approval of performing artists and writers. Perhaps it was this marketing switch that opened the doors for the long and varied trail of rock and roll musicians that arose from the 1960s.

Rock and roll music and the dances it spawned underwent many changes during the turbulent '60s, as new styles were introduced by the Beatles and the Rolling Stones, and many other bands imported to the U.S. from London. The twist set the ground rules—anything goes—for the dances of the 1960s, and remained popular for several years. Teens twisted at sock hops, while jet-setters were storming hot spots like New York's Peppermint Lounge. For a time, the club was so popular that dancers adopted the Peppermint twist. Everyone could identify with the free and percussive movements of the twist and rock and roll music. It didn't take training by the dancers—just nerve. Eventually, everyone was out on the dance floor again.

The dances of the 1960s were as diverse as the bands that hit the recording industry. A slew of them hit America within just a few years—the Watusi, the pony, the boogaloo, the frug, the funky Broadway, the slop, the mashed potato, the monkey, the hitchhiker, the swim, the shake, the skate and dozens of others. Men and women still danced together, generally, but the new dances discouraged touching and encouraged individuality.

Rock, jazz, blues, country and western, bluegrass and folk music joined the original rock and roll style, and as young people experimented with nondancing music, dancing became less popular at private parties. The peak of the hippie generation and the anti-war protests of students gave a new bent to popular music. Once again, emphasis was placed on lyrics, and on the message that a song expressed, rather than on its rhythm. The drug-oriented counterculture, along with the rock concert, encouraged listening, and dance took a back seat as far as youth was concerned.

The dance that was popular was quite informal. People danced in everything from blue jeans and T-shirts to peasant dresses and overalls. Often, "dancing" was nothing more than swaying to the beat of the band featured at a rock concert. With the trend toward listening to music, the light shows and new sound amplification techniques of the 1960s helped the rock concert flourish. The shows became more and more elaborate, and those who tired of viewing rather than participating flocked to the first discotheques of the 1960s. Imported from the French Riviera to New York, the discos enjoyed a brief flurry of popularity before yielding again to the rock concerts. Famous spots such as Arthur's, Yellow Fingers and Cheetah are a few that managed to survive in New York.

In the meantime, the rock concert concept was carried to the extreme, with complicated acts put on by artists like Alice Cooper, Lou Reed, David Bowie and others. In the mid-1970s, the music and record-buying crowd split. Those who chose to continue to be part of the audience favored glitter or punk rock. Those who tired of the sidelines took to the disco dance floor and started a phenomenon unique to the dance world. Participation was in; watching was out.

2
THE DISCO SOUND

The disco sound is immediately recognizable and unforgettable. It's old and new, and it comes in various styles and rhythmic patterns. But whatever its form, it is a sound that captivates you and demands that you dance.

The worldwide magic that prompted the resurgence of discotheques and dancing is, however, not just another passing style of music to be pressed into plastic and played on a stereo set. In fact, the disco sound, while a part of the whole discomania trend, is actually a phenomenon in its own right which has affected many other media forms and business markets.

The English translation of *Discotheque* is *record library:* recorded music is essential to disco dancing. So, obviously, it is in the recording industry that we see one of the greatest examples of disco's influence. Recording companies have experienced booming sales of disco hits, with labels like Casablanca making a smash with their emphasis on disco recordings.

Discomania really has revolutionized the recording industry. The trend has affected the type of music that is recorded, as well as the type of disc and the way the various tunes find their way to the top of the charts. In recent years, hits were born on the radio. Today, many of them are born in the disco clubs. Traditionally, radio disc jockeys decided which new music would be introduced to their listeners. If the listening—and buying—response was favorable, or if the DJ really felt he had found a winner, the song would receive more and more air time as it climbed the charts. The important point, however, is that it was the radio disc jockey who decided initially whether a song would be given the chance to become a hit.

With the advent of disco came a new sequence of events in the making of a recording hit. As disco dancing—and the clubs and music—gained popularity, recording companies started producing long-playing records meant for dancing. These are now available to the public in many retail record stores. But the true disco disc is a 12-inch, 18-minute version of the two- and three-minute song played on the radio, and is produced specifically for use in the disco clubs. The main feature of these discs is their high quality, suitable for use with the sophisticated sound systems of the discotheques, and capable of eliminating sound distortion problems at high volumes.

In today's recording industry, the disco club often receives the first copy of a new tune, serving as the testing ground for new recordings. Producers like the instant reaction of the disco crowd and are using the situation to test and promote not only new songs, but new ideas and concepts in disco sound. Generally, if a club's DJ likes a new song, he will try it out on the dancers, who in turn will let him know whether or not they like it. If they do, they demand to hear it more and more. Thus, it is up to the radio disc jockey to find out what the dancers and listeners prefer. So it is quite likely that a song has already become popular in the disco clubs before you ever hear it on the radio. For instance, 100,000 copies of the single hit "Get Dancin'" were sold in the recording's first six weeks before it had any air play at all. The song, recorded by Disco Tex and the Sexolettes (actually Monty Rock III backed up by a group of studio musicians), broke at New York's Le Jardin, and then was performed at discos across the country. Other clubs—and DJs—take great pride in being able to say, "you heard it here first," especially if the club can take credit for the song's hit status. This turnaround in the making of hits has put the dancers in a position of even more control where popular music is concerned than they had during the earlier years of rock.

The result of this revolution? The dancers are calling for more of the same in disco sounds. In fact, some rock and roll purists feel that this control by the public has stifled the creativity of performing and recording artists, forcing them to pump out disc after disc of the same rhythm patterns and basic melodies. But, regardless of such criticism, the dancers and listeners are more than satisfied with the disco sounds being produced. If and when they do change their tastes in dancing music they will surely let the recording industry know about it, just as they have in the past.

In one way, music lovers of all ilks have benefited from disco's effect on radio programming. The nonstop music that plays in the disco clubs has turned listeners into a more demanding bunch, who want that trend to continue when they flip on their radios. Consequently, many pop AM radio stations have followed the lead of their FM counterparts, playing uninterruped music for long stretches of air time.

The disco sound has crept into the other media offerings as well as radio. Movies like *Saturday Night Fever* and *Thank God It's Friday* have not only attracted many viewers on the strength of their soundtracks, they have also spurred dramatic record sales of the soundtrack albums. On television, viewers also have been treated to many looks at the disco scene. Longstanding music-and-dance programs like *American Bandstand* and *Soul Train* picked up on the disco trend immediately, as did weekend rock-and-roll shows like the *Midnight Special.*

Close behind these trendsetters were a wide spectrum of American talk shows.

Merv Griffin's televised disco dance special from Caesar's Palace in Las Vegas grabbed one of the highest ratings ever received by the long-running variety talk show. Phil Donahue presented his disco special from Chicago and Mike Douglas introduced audiences to the West Coast entertainment.

While Dinah Shore consistently presented disco artists on her daytime talk show, Johnny Carson jumped on the bandwagon via nighttime TV. Even the news-oriented "60 Minutes" has examined the world of disco.

On the commercial end of television, viewers have been treated to advertisements for disco lessons, recordings of disco music and disco practice and exercise aids. In fact, commercial slots advertising products that have nothing to do with disco or dancing have adopted a disco theme in the hope of attracting viewers' attention.

The other forms of art and entertainment also have been affected by discomania. Back in 1975, Van McCoy staged a disco show at New York City's Avery Fisher Hall, complete with string section and disco dancers. And just as rock and roll influences crept into Broadway shows and other dance programs, disco is bound to appear eventually in the repertoires of modern and jazz dance companies.

Trademarks of Disco Music

No matter how much variety you encounter in disco music, there is always that common denominator—rhythm. Those who describe a disco tune by saying, "It has a good beat; you can dance to it,'' are not far from pinpointing the essence of the sound.

Basically, disco music combines strings and big-band effects to come up with foot-stomping, hip-bumping, happy music that almost forces you to get up and move. The disco sound can be called one of the latest forms of rock and roll (see history of rock and roll in Chapter 1). It can even be traced back to influences that were evident in the music played for dancers of the jitterbug, the Charleston and the other lively dances of the past.

But the rhythms of disco music are stronger and more erotic than the rhythms of its predecessors. And the ethnic spirit behind the songs is more powerful than ever before in American popular music. Remember that disco movements are earthy, and no matter how sophisticated the entire musical arrangement, the rhythm is simple and deeply rooted in the rhythms of age-old cultures. For instance, just like the dance steps, much of the music heard in the disco clubs is Latin through and through. Other numbers, harking back to the soul and Motown styles of the 1960s, are based heavily on African and American Black rhythms.

While the radio version of a particular recording may feature a short repetition of the basic melody and beat, the disco club version mixes long rhythm sections with melodic interludes and generally negligible lyrics. No matter which type of digression the song makes, however, that driving beat is always there.

One testimony to the fact that disco is an established form of entertainment rather than just a passing fad is that the music has been adapted to the styles of just about every major ethnic group in the U.S. Many looked at the sound as a black-only trend, in which members of other races would be out of place. This idea proved to be false, as the Latin Hustle quickly followed the basic Hustle onto the dance floor, and the all-white Bee Gees became a phenomenal disco success throughout the world.

The differences between styles of disco music are often faint. Once they have been swept up by that urge to dance, few enthusiasts care about the ethnic flavor or the other variations from one song to the next. The beat is the important thing. However, disco styles are as diverse as were the styles of folk, blues and

rock music in the 1960s. And with the number of new artists to storm the recording industry, today, the dancer and/or listener has many styles and variations to choose from.

Roots of the Rhythm— History of the Disco Sound

Most aficionados will agree that it was Van McCoy who solidified the disco sound revolution with his smash-hit recording of ''The Hustle.'' When this catchy, instrumental song, written, arranged and performed by McCoy, was introduced to the public in 1975, it became an instant hit. Soon, the song was Number One on all the charts. *The New York Times* called it the biggest dance recording of the 1970s, and the National Academy of Recording Arts and Sciences gave the song its Grammy Award for Best Pop Instrumental cut.

Perhaps it was timing that really made McCoy's song a hit. According to the artist, he had never even seen the dance performed when the first glimmerings of the song took form in his mind. But McCoy, who had earlier produced and promoted recordings by such well known pop veterans as Gladys Knight and the Pips, the Shirelles and Aretha Franklin, was no stranger to market foresight, and he made it his business to discover the hustle and release his song with perfect timing.

In 1974 and early 1975, the hustle was just beginning to take hold in New York City and other dance centers. Not only did the dance's popularity push the song's popularity, but the song itself furthered the hustle dance. In fact, some people still think that McCoy himself invented the hustle dance.

It really is difficult to pinpoint some exact event that started the disco music boom, and even if you choose Van McCoy's recording of ''The Hustle'' as such a turning point, disco music can be traced back farther in rock's history. Actually, it could be said that it was the dancers who initiated disco music. At first, they merely chose which tunes they liked to dance to, and as musicians and composers became aware of this trend, they began to try to create the sound that dancers were seeking.

It was almost inevitable that the music chosen by dancers was the most modern version of soul music. Throughout the 1960s, music recorded on the Motown label was played at parties for dancing. The dance steps were totally unprescribed, but most dancers found the driving beat of the Supremes, the Four Tops, Smokey Robinson and the Miracles, Stevie Wonder and other famous soul artists the best rhythms to dance to.

As dancing increased in popularity while rock concerts fell by the wayside, new tunes became more and more oriented toward dancing. Two of the earliest artists to produce music stamped with the disco sound were Barry White and Gloria Gaynor. Gaynor's ''Never Can Say Goodbye'' and ''How High the Moon,'' plus White's ''Can't Get Enough of Your Love, Babe'' and ''Love's Theme'' became instant disco hits. And after Van McCoy started the ball rolling, many old soul bands experienced renewed success with disco tunes. Such veteran groups as the Isley Brothers, the O'Jays, the Spinners and the Originals were back at the top of the charts, thanks to disco. Other soul stalwarts, such as James Brown, have also taken to the disco scene with hit singles and long-playing albums galore.

Ask a discomaniac which music he likes best, and you're likely to hear the names of the Trammps, the Commodores, Chic, Brass Construction, and of course, the Bee Gees. The progressive rock sounds of artists like Boz Scaggs also can be heard on the dance floor. In contrast to the modern sounds are big-band hits of the past which many dancers now swear by. And for anyone who believes that the disco sound is really limited, take note of the fact that you might even hear the melodies of avant garde rocker David Bowie played after the renovated tunes of 1950s rock-and-roller Frankie Valli on the disco floor.

Make no mistake about it: Disco dancers *will* demand a good beat, but they will never turn down a rhythmic tune on the basis of who the artist is. Some dancers, of course, prefer a particular type of sound, many of them choosing to buy records with the Latin, or Salsa, sound. Salsa is the Spanish word for sauce, and you probably won't find anything spicier in recordings or dancing than this Latin style. The recipe for this disco gravy calls for driving hip movements, an irresistible beat and that ethnic electricity you can find only in the melt-

ing-pot metropolises of the U.S. The Salsa sound is produced by groups like the SalSoul and Tito Puente Orchestras, among others.

For some discomaniacs, there's nothing better to dance to than the soundtracks of movies like *Saturday Night Fever and Thank God It's Friday,* with their varied selection of tunes and popular artists. Again, many viewers went to see *Thank God It's Friday* for no other reason than to hear the musical creations of the Commodores and Donna Summer.

Van McCoy's recording of The Hustle, *introduced in 1975, was instrumental in the disco revolution. (Courtesy Roy Radin Associates)*

The Isley Brothers—a veteran rock group with a long list of hits behind them—adapted to disco style with considerable success. (Courtesy Epic Records)

Along with Donna Summer, many other new artists have cropped up and are cashing in on discomania. Linda Clifford, Andy Gibb (the youngest of the Gibbs Brothers, who form the Bee Gees) and Michael Zager are among them, with new musicians introduced all the time. Another popular artist in America and in Europe is Cerrone, a French musician who produces, writes and performs on his own top disco albums. Cerrone has been credited with great contributions to the disco world. At the 1978 Disco Forum IV held in New York City, Cerrone picked up awards for male disco artist of the year, disco music arranger of the year, disco instrumentalist of the year, disco composer of the year (for ''Cerrone III/Supernature''), and best producer of a disco record (for three different albums).

Where is it all going? Many onlookers of the

Singer and actress Donna Summer's career was given a big boost by the movie Thank God It's Friday. (Courtesy Casablanca Record and FilmWorks)

music world feel the rock and roll sound of the 1960s and early 1970s has split into two factions or styles: disco music on the one hand, and punk or new wave rock on the other. The truth is that in many recent cases, the two have merged—witness David Bowie's music driving disco dancers to the floor in droves. There is no telling whether this trend will continue. Disco music may continue to borrow from new wave rock to keep itself alive and growing. Or the two may be separated by an even greater rift in style. Whatever the outcome, however, the disco sound is likely to be around for quite a while.

The Personality Behind the Scenes—The DJ

The discotheque's disc jockey plays a supremely important role in the rise and fall of disco tunes. But, in the overall ambiance and success of a disco club, the disc jockey is

Cerrone — a European musician with a considerable following on both sides of the Atlantic — has found great success recording disco-style albums. (Courtesy Cotillion Records)

A disc jockey is responsible for the overall sound and pace of music played in a disco.

Boz Scaggs' 1976 album titled Silk Degrees *combined his R&B background with the new disco sound for a triple-platinum success. (Courtesy Columbia Records)*

even more powerful. So powerful, in fact, that the DJ can actually make or break a disco club. It is up to the disc jockey to set the mood of the club and control the dancers. Essentially, the DJ is Master of Ceremonies at the discotheque. He or she runs the dance contests, takes musical requests and hints from the dancers, and does everything possible to instill the fever in the club's patrons. The DJ must know when to build the crowd to a dramatic frenzy and when to cool the dancers down.

To accomplish this, the DJ plays records in building succession, making it almost impossible for the dancers to consider leaving the floor. And even with the help of computerized turntables which put on music with the same number of beats per minute to make each song flow into the next, the DJ must be highly skilled in his art. The DJ uses sophisticated

segueing and beat-counting techniques and must incorporate pinpoint timing. Usually, the DJ wears headphones so that he can begin listening to a new song while the current number is still playing. Usually, the DJ will not play an entire song all the way through, but rather, will switch to a new one in a manner that makes the songs flow smoothly. This, and the ability to judge the energy levels of the dancers, is what makes one disc jockey better than another. Through his control of the music and dancers, the DJ inevitably interjects his own personality into the club. Consequently, in many cities, particular DJs have developed their own following of dancers who will move from club to club as the DJ moves.

Many disc jockeys also hold day jobs, but their disco employment is hardly a second job to them. Most of them take their disco duties quite seriously, some giving up daytime jobs when disco becomes more profitable and more fulfilling. It is not unusual for the DJ to be credited with gold records when he introduces a song that later becomes a smash. Like everything else in the disco world, the DJs are becoming highly competitive, as the clubs vie for the best disc jockeys and the DJs seek the best jobs, often those in private, exclusive clubs. By 1978 the DJ had become such a common figure in the job market that DJs began to talk union. Whether or not the union idea will take hold is uncertain.

Whether it's Latin or soul, big-band or new-wave, the disco sound is the sound of today. You'll hear it on the radio, television and the stage, in films and, of course, in any disco club. Choose the style you prefer, and try to pick out the rhythm. It won't take long before the beat begins to surge through your mind and body, and you'll feel that irresistible urge to move.

3
THE FIRST STEP:
Warm-ups and Isolations

Discomania is on the uprise, and it seems that just about everyone is catching the fever. Eager dancers, decked out in their Saturday Night Finest, line up at the doors of popular city discos. And thousands of enthusiasts are taking dance lessons. Disco dancing now attracts people of all ages. The publishing, film and recording industries are promoting this phenomenon with a fervor never before seen in the dance world. Disco dancing really is for everyone, but because they've never tried it, there are still many who avoid the dance floor. To a first-time spectator, the flashing lights, electric colors, and twirling figures can be overwhelming. And in many discos, the stage is set so well that the onlooker may be intimidated.

One aim of this book is to show skeptics that they can leave the disco sidelines and participate—regardless of age or sex. The complex dances that look like they would take years to master are just a series of much simpler steps. In this chapter, we give a complete warm-up regimen to follow. Based on disco dance fundamentals and body isolations, these exercises are meant to relax you, tone up your muscles and bring your energy to its peak. They should be done before you go out on Saturday night to limber you up for the dance floor, but they also can be used as a regular exercise routine to keep you physically fit. The bonus is that they actually are fun to do, and a good session will make you feel like you've just had a professional massage.

Just as importantly, the exercises are designed around the most basic movements used in common disco dance steps. Once you have mastered each part of the routine, you have all the elements of disco dancing. Another extra provided by these exercises is the self-confidence they can instill. By doing them, you will become more comfortable with your body and the movements it is capable of executing. The more you do the exercises, the fuller your movements become, and the greater and freer your range of movement. With practice, the moves that once seemed like impossible contortions can become automatic to you.

The first step in moving easily is to realize that you *can* move. However obvious that may seem, many of us are not fully aware of the potential our muscles hold. Movement is the most natural ability that we have. One of the first things the newborn child does is to *learn to move,* and as he grows, he *moves in order to learn.* Perhaps it is only later that we forget that natural ability.

Disco could be described as the rebirth of that awareness throughout the world. Coming as a natural followup to the nutrition- and fitness-conscious trends of today, it gives individuals a chance to combine healthy exercise with recreation.

Besides reviving your movement skills, the exercises in this chapter should prove once and for all that everyone has rhythm. Sometimes the star athlete who breaks records on the basketball court on Saturday afternoon balks at the dance floor when the sun goes down because he insists he has no rhythm. The idea of performing the simplest step to music can chill the very bones of the most stoical jock.

Actually, the athlete often does find dancing difficult because he or she has already developed and trained large muscle groups to perform particular movement patterns. The dancer, on the other hand, needs to move individual muscles or smaller muscle groups, as in the isolations in this chapter. Ultimately, the athlete can become the best dancer because he or she already has developed a kinesthetic awareness (understanding of muscles in movement). At our dance center, we hold all-male classes for athletes interested in developing their sports potential through dance... but we'll save that for another book. The point is that the block is often mental as well as physical. Uninitiated students have even told us that they thought they had to be able to sing to be able to dance.

No one really knows how, why or when rhythm is transformed into an alien entity for some people. Somehow a mental block is erected, or the rhythm that is an essential part of the universe is buried so deeply within us that we cannot hear it. Rhythm exists on every level of the world, from the rising and setting of the sun to the ebb and flow of the tides. It is as natural as our own heartbeats and breaths. With the help of these exercises, you will rediscover an awareness of rhythm.

It takes only a few peaceful minutes to sit down and pick out the various rhythms around you. We would be exaggerating, however, if we said, "You, too, can dance like John Tra-

volta in 24 hours." Like anything else, dancing must be learned one step at a time. And no matter how quickly you progress, you have to start at the beginning. If you're out of shape, you might as well count on doing the exercise routine in its entirety several times. If you feel comfortable with some of the moves, spend more time on the ones that seem more difficult to you. Above all, don't be discouraged if you feel sore, or if you can't quite do all the movements the first time around. Just keep in mind that once you've stimulated a particular muscle, it can be stimulated again. In effect, you're awakening your muscles, and regular exercise will keep them from going back into hibernation.

If you play tennis three times a week, and jog five miles a day, accomplishing the movements in this chapter may seem like child's play. In that case, concentrate on improving the quality of your movements by keeping *each part of your body* well tuned. If you're superbly physically fit, you might want to devote your exercise sessions to perfecting your rhythm. Practicing these exercises also helps you develop the disco style and look. If for no other reason, using these exercises to warm up before a Saturday night outing will prevent the pangs of morning-after soreness.

Before you start, try to achieve an optimistic frame of mind. Tell yourself that you *can* move. The methods and sequence of these exercises are based on secrets used by professional dancers, and devised by us through our experiences with students. Don't be alarmed. Technical terms are few and far between and the movements are hardly formidable.

In general, the series of movements is based on a technique called isolation, which is exactly what you would expect it to be. Isolations are movements separating one part of your body from the remainder, and moving only that part. This helps you become aware of the movements each part is capable of, and the muscles that control those movements. Isolations also serve to loosen tension, since each exercise focuses on one muscle, making sure it is stretched and relaxed before moving on to the next.

The exercises start with the head and proceed to the toes. This sequence is important because much of our tension is felt in the head and neck area. By relaxing those muscles first, you make it easier for the rest of your body to comply. To some extent, the movements also progress in difficulty, so that each prepares you for the next.

One of the most helpful tricks to making the movement you desire is to aid yourself with visual images. For example, imagine that you are creating a design in space when you dance. Most of the moves in disco dancing—or in any other type of dancing—can be defined by some sort of familiar shape. When you swing your hips all the way around, you're drawing a circle in the air with your hips. In some exercises, you are creating parallel, diagonal or perpendicular lines between the floor and a part of your body. Concentrating on these factors will help you accomplish the desired effect.

It also helps to associate the movement you are making with another, more familiar movement. For instance, you might be able to do a head swing more easily if you imagine yourself being slapped in the face—sans pain, of course. Or, to make a complete and smooth circle with your head, you can picture your head inside a hat box, with the top of the head brushing against its sides.

Another thing to keep in mind while exercising is the nature of disco dancing. Unlike the waltz or other longstanding ballroom dances, disco steps are percussive and sharply defined. Where the waltz is soft and fluid, disco is dynamic and rhythmic. Don't let that frighten you away; disco is also joyful and invigorating. You're almost guaranteed to be swept up by the music and the beat.

This brings us to the actual preparations you should make before starting these exercises. There are, in fact, very few. You don't need an exercise mat, a gymnasium, ballet slippers or a fancy leotard. What you do need is your own body and enough space to give you free movement at arm's length. Your sense of relaxation will hardly improve if you insist on warming up among Grandma's priceless antiques, but you really don't need very much space.

For clothing, wear what is comfortable for you. The only criterion is that the clothing should allow free movement everywhere. As for your feet, it's best to go barefoot, at least at first. If you really prefer to wear shoes, choose a pair that offers your foot and ankle

good support and, again, comfort. Going without shoes, however, allows you to feel the floor more closely and gives you a stronger base support.

Try doing the exercise in front of a full-length mirror so you can check your progress. Or warm up with a friend, and you can advise each other.

The final, and possibly most important, ingredient is music. Since you'll be dancing to music once you venture into the discos, you might as well start at home. The only thing you should consider seriously in choosing the music is how you react to it. Flip on your radio or record player and tune in something that appeals to you, that makes you want to move. After all, dance is music in motion.

To preface the actual exercise, turn on the music and then sit down and relax. Close your eyes if it helps you concentrate on the music. Try to pick out the bass rhythm, since this is the beat that you will dance to, and let the beat surge through you. The fact that you'll probably end up tapping your feet or clapping your hands proves how automatically rhythm comes to us if we open up to it. When you feel like moving to the beat, you're ready to begin.

To keep the rhythm going constantly in your mind, do the exercises that follow in series of eight beats. Most disco music is based on eight-count phrases, so this will help you get accustomed to the music. Where the exercise requires a right and left limb or a right and left motion, you can perfect your rhythm by alternating sides and moving according to the following sequence of 32 counts: eight beats to the right, eight to the left; four to the right and four to the left; two to the right and two to the left; finally, a series of single beats in the sequence right, left, right, left.

Right	Left
Eight	Eight
Four	Four
Two	Two
One	One
One	One

For those movements that do not lend themselves to this system, just repeat the movements as you desire, counting out eight beats.

THE EXERCISES
THE ABCs OF DANCE

With your mind turned away from office problems or the mess your children made with their crayons on your newly scrubbed floor, stand up straight but relaxed with your feet parallel and close together. You should feel comfortable, balanced and firmly, but not immovably, anchored to the floor.

Head Isolations

In today's disco, moving the head is as important as moving the arms or legs. Keep in mind that *every part of your body must learn to dance.* When you practice the isolations that follow, imagine that your head—or any other single part of your body—is dancing on its own. Once you have mastered each isolation, your whole body will be ready to dance. The following exercises, done by themselves, will release a lot of tension that builds up in the head and neck. Remember what the word isolation means, and concentrate on moving *only* the head or neck.

Head Tilt. Start in the same position as for the head turn, but drop your head to the right, as if you were trying to touch your ear to your shoulder. Do not lift your shoulder to meet your ear. Let the weight of your head do the work, and your neck muscles will thank you for it.

This is a movement that you probably don't do in your everyday activities, so don't be surprised if you feel a slight tension as you stretch the neck muscles.

Head Drop. With your head in the same starting position, drop your head forward, your chin falling to your chest. Then raise your head and drop it backward. Repeat these motions until they feel comfortable, practicing to eight beats. Start out slowly and gradually increase your energy level. Your ultimate goal is to snap your head into the upright position on the return from each drop. This move, like most disco moves, should be executed with dynamics.

Head Turn. With feet together and body straight but relaxed, look forward. Turn your head to the right, to the front again, and to the left. Move only your head, without tilting it forward or backward. Once you've done this several times, try a sequence of 32 beats as described earlier: eight turns to the right, eight to the left; four turns to the right, four to the left; two turns to the right, two turns to the left; one to the right and one to the left; another to the right and another turn to the left. Keep a steady, constant beat.

Head Swing. This is an attractive and common disco move. Again, the trick is in snapping your head from one position to the next. Begin with your head dropped forward, chin on chest. In one motion, swing your head toward the right, hitting the back of your head on an imaginary wall behind you. The snapping motion will return you to the original position. Now swing your head up and out to the left. With all three positions forming one smooth motion, your head traces an arc in space, like a huge smile. You may hear sort of a crackling or grinding noise in your neck when you do this. Do not despair: it means only that you haven't used those muscles in a while. Practice this to eight beats and add your own flair.

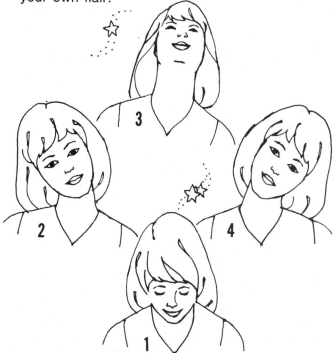

Head Rotation. This combines all the previous movements. In a rotation, the part of your body that is isolated draws a circle in the air. Start with your head dropped forward, and turn it smoothly to the right, backward, to the left, and forward again. Try not to cheat on this one; while it sounds simple, we've found that a lot of beginners cannot make a complete circle with their head. To accomplish a full rotation, be sure that you are looking toward the ceiling as you drop your head back. If it helps, imagine that you are drawing a circle in space with your eyes. You'll be glad you did—this is the best alternative to a masseur that we know. Don't be one sided; reverse the rotation by starting to the left.

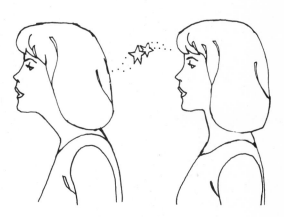

Chin Thrust. This is a slightly comical, well-known move often associated with East Indian dancing. Today, it is linked to funky disco dancing. We tell our students to picture a turtle poking its head in and out of the shell. Start with your head erect, and jut your chin straight out in front of you. Your shoulders should be still and your jawline parallel with the floor. Move back to the original position and continue the motion to eight beats.

Shoulder Isolations

The ball-and-socket joint that forms the shoulder is capable of a lot of movement, much of it coming into play in disco dance styling. The trick in the following exercises is to truly isolate your shoulders, letting your arms hang limp and follow through naturally from the shoulder's lead.

Shoulder Shrug. This is exactly what it sounds like. Ignoring the head, lift both shoulders simultaneously toward your ears. Push them down again, and practice the whole movement to eight slow beats, followed by eight fast beats.

Shoulder Tilt. In this exercise, the shoulders work alternately. Raise your right shoulder while lowering the left. The motion is like a child's teeter-totter. Let your arms be pulled by the shoulders. Practice this to eight slow beats, followed by eight fast beats.

Full Shoulder Rotation. This exercise is based on the same concept as is the head rotation. However, it's complicated by one extra factor: the arms are firmly attached to the shoulders. Thus, you will have to make a little extra effort to concentrate on the shoulders and ignore the arms. To make it easier, try first doing a backstroke motion with both arms, just as if you were swimming. Now try the same motion with your arms hanging limp, so that your shoulders do the work, and your arms merely go along for the ride. Don't let your arms fly up and away from your body. As in the head rotation, be sure to complete a smooth circle with your shoulders. You can reverse the rotation by trying a forward butterfly swim stroke and then continuing the forward shoulder motion without the arms.

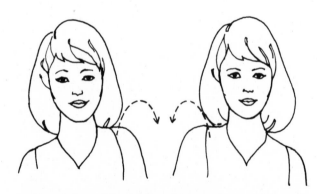

Alternating Shoulder Rotation. In this rotation, the shoulders oppose each other in position. While the right shoulder is at the lowest point on the circle, the left shoulder is at the highest point. You can do this rotation forward or backward, as in the full shoulder rotation. Try this in an alternating, left-right series.

Shimmy. This is the familiar shoulder-shaking move that has been around for a long time and is still a rage on the disco scene. Starting slowly to establish a steady rhythm, thrust one shoulder forward, and then the other. This is basically the same movement as in the shoulder tilt, but forward and backward, rather than up and down. When the right shoulder is forward, the left shoulder is back, and vice versa. Build your speed on the shimmy by practicing to eight beats and increasing the tempo.

After you practice the preceding exercises, your head and shoulders are ready to dance. Before moving on to the arm isolations, try mixing some of the exercises. For instance, you can try alternating the head turn with the shoulder shrug. Or, go a step further and try doing a head isolation simultaneously with a shoulder isolation. This should begin to give you the feeling of true dancing, as one part moves in conjunction, or harmony, with another. At this point, you might want to change the music you've chosen. This is not absolutely necessary, but it will make you more comfortable with varying tempos that you will encounter on the dance floor. It can also revive your interest and energy during the exercises.

For the next series of exercises, your feet should be moved to the open stance. In other words, spread your feet about a foot apart, or at whatever distance is comfortable for you. You should feel like you are planted firmly on the floor.

Arm Isolations

The movements you make with your arms determine whether your dancing is sophisticated or funky. The arms can often be the focus for individual expression on the dance floor, so it is important that you know how to move them in every way possible. This is especially important to couple dancing, where peak mobility is essential.

Most of the following movements use the full length of the arm and, consequently, the shoulder, which just cannot help moving to some extent as well. At this point, ignore your hands, for they will only distract you from isolating the arm. If it helps, curl your fingers, as if you were holding some coins in your palms. This should keep your hands out of sight and mind for the arm isolations.

The Pull Back. This is another well-used movement on the disco floor, and has been subject to many variations. To get the basic motion down, start with your wrists crossed in front of your chest to form a letter X. Again, curl your fingers so they won't distract you.

Hold your elbows at a comfortable, relaxed angle. To begin the exercise, uncross your wrists as you extend your arms out to the front. *Don't push the arms out straight; the arms should be bent slightly throughout the exercise.* Still bent, swing your arms out to the side and then to the rear. Swoop them downward and then up again to the crossed-wrist position. This is a pulling back movement similar to rowing a boat. Practice this to eight beats. For variety, try this movement with the shimmy.

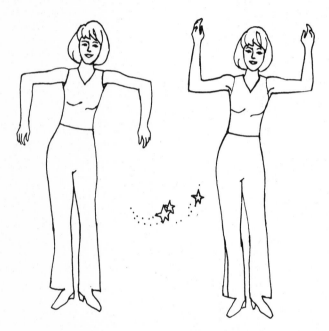

Forearm Swing. This exercise calls up the image of a scarecrow hung in a cornfield from a stake and crossbar. Lift your elbows up and out to bring your upper arms into a parallel position with the floor. We tell our students to try to imagine hanging their elbows over the crossbar. Let your forearms hang straight down, relaxed. Swing your forearms back and forth, with your elbows as the pivot points, so that your hands or fingers point toward the ceiling and then down to the floor. For variety, alternate arms—one arm swinging back as the other swings forward.

Arm Thrust. This, too, is a common disco movement. Forgetting the rest of your body, throw your right arm up to point to the corner of the room. Flexing your wrists as if you are blocking the sun from your eyes, push against an imaginary ceiling with your upturned palm. Be sure to flex your elbow to accomplish a good thrusting action, and stay aware of your stopping point. Try this with each arm individually, and then in the 32-count series described on page 25.

Full Arm Swing. Stand straight with your arms hanging loose. Using your whole arm, swing both arms to the right. Follow through with your fingers stretched to the highest possible point and your weight as far to the right as possible without falling. Your arms should remain roughly parallel. The arms draw an arc in space, swinging from the right, down, and through to the left side The downswing should cause your legs to bend, and momentum will help you follow through. Reverse the swing starting from the left side.

Wrist Isolation

The following exercise helps you flex and extend your wrist to its maximum potential.

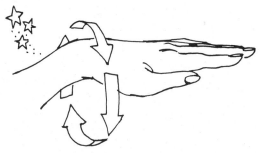

Wrist Rotation. Keep your fingers straight but relaxed, and simply make a rotation with the wrist. You can do this with both hands simultaneously.

Hand Isolations

Every part of the body must enter the harmony of rhythm when you dance. We have found that many dancers who have perfected the hip, head and other movements have no idea of what to do with their hands. To a great extent, this is a matter of creativity. Dance is expression as well as form and you should generally do what feels and looks best to you. The following are a few of the basic possibilities which also offer good stretching motion.

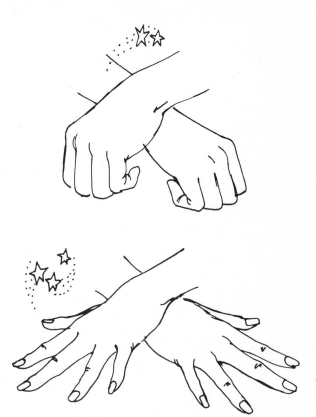

The Finger Burst. This exercise works the hand muscles, and is quite easy to do. Clench your fist, and then quickly release the fingers to a fully extended position. To make the movement as sharp as it should be, imagine yourself shouting, "Zap!" and lighting all the lamps in the room with your open fingers. With both hands, try this zapping with your wrists crossed, and then try zapping your hands out to the side. Practice to eight beats to get used to the move.

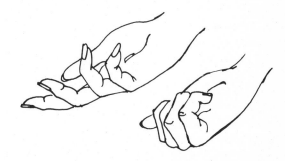

The Beckoning Hand. We often associate this move with a gesture popularized by gypsies, but it has roots in Spain and India as well. Turn your palms up and keep your fingers extended but relaxed. One by one, bring your fingers in to touch the palm, starting with the little finger and proceeding to the index finger. Practice the movement to four beats with the right hand and four with the left.

At this point, you've completed another stage in your dance education. Now your arms and hands should be able to dance along with your head and shoulders. Hopefully, you have experienced a new awareness of your movement potential. If you wish, take a break and change your music again.

Torso and Waist Isolations

Mastering the following isolations is of the utmost importance to a dancer. Disco dancing takes advantage of every muscle you have, including those which move your hips, torso and waist. This part of your body is much more than a base of operations for your versatile limbs. As such, it should be given equal time and effort.

All you need to do to recognize the importance of your middle in disco dancing is to watch someone on the dance floor. The hips bump, the waist twists and the stomach or diaphragm area pulses in and out in time with the music. If these areas don't move, your style will be stiff and robot-like. You don't have to be a veteran belly dancer to accomplish these effects, but you do have to practice to achieve the percussive, strutting motions inherent in disco dancing.

It is difficult to actually isolate one part of the torso from the others, for the connection between them is much more solid than between the neck and shoulders or the arm and hand. There are no ball-and-socket joints here, so you might have to depend a bit more on your mental powers at first to isolate the various parts. It might help you succeed to remember how much extra weight is located here. In this area is your center of gravity, and you'll need a little extra push to move the same distance. The focal point for most of these exercises is the waist or spine; their proximity to your center of gravity will require extra stability during the movements. To avoid toppling over in the middle of a waist rotation or body swing, plant both feet firmly on the floor; you'll get maximum waist action from this extra support.

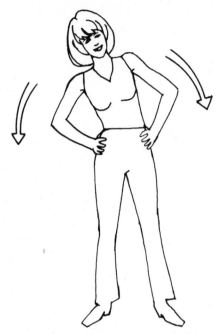

Side Stretch. Stand up straight and rest your hands on your hips. Now drop your torso to the right side from the waist. Do not move the torso forward or backward, only directly to the side. Still bent to the side, bounce slightly to eight percussive beats as if your head is nailing an object to your side. You should feel this exercise pulling at your thigh and waist muscles. Practice this to a series of eight, four, two and one beats, left to right.

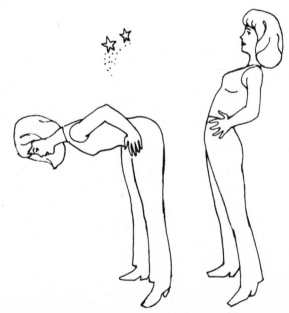

Forward and Backward Stretch. With hands on hips and legs straight, bend forward until your back forms a flat table parallel to the floor. Do eight percussive beats forward, keeping your neck straight. Again, imagine nailing an object near the floor with your forhead. Now stand up straight, look at the ceiling, arch your back and pulse backward eight times. You should feel this motion pulling your abdominal muscles.

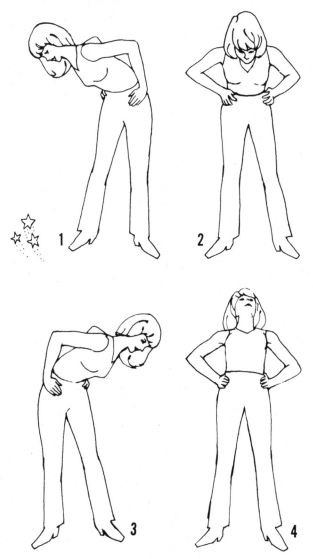

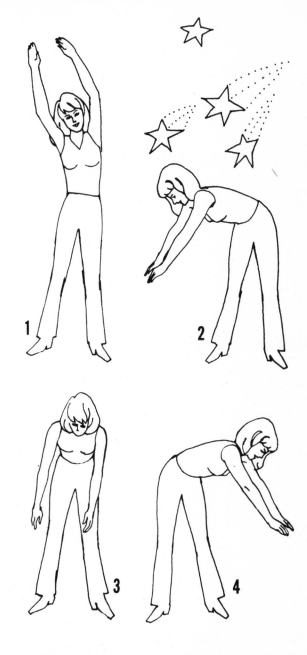

Waist Rotation. Combining the exercises above, rotate the upper half of your body from the waist. To make a circle with the torso, concentrate on your waist and everything else will follow through.

Full Body Swing. In this exercise, the whole torso swoops down from the waist, creating an arc as in the head and arm swings. Start with your arms extended above you, swinging them to the right; stretch a little and swoop downward to the side. Relax through this motion; the weight of your body will carry your torso to the left and up again to complete a full circle in the air. If you really let yourself go, this exercise is exhilarating.

Torso Twist. Lift your elbows up and out to the side, turn your palms up and bring them in toward your chest until the fingertips meet. With your feet firmly anchored to the floor, twist the entire torso right and left sideways with energy. Imagine that you're trying to look far behind you.

Body Contraction. This is an unusual part of the exercise routine, but if you watch a

dancer, you'll discover that it is an integral part of disco. As we mentioned earlier, the middle section of your body really does dance along with the rest. In this particular movement, your stomach and diaphragm area actually dances. The contraction is a forceful, hard movement that plays an important part in the strut characteristic of many disco steps. It is especially powerful because the adjacent limbs cannot help being pulled in by the contraction.

Again, this movement is exactly what you would expect it to be. In a contraction, the center of your body caves in, pulling your arms and neck in toward it. Your chest is pulled in sharply, pushing your back out slightly, and pulling your shoulders and head down toward the diaphragm. The best way to imitate this move is to picture yourself being punched in the stomach, however unappealing the thought. If it helps, draw in your breath sharply. Repeat the exercise more quickly by contracting and releasing the muscles to eight beats. Once you have mastered this, try emphasizing the isolation by contracting without using the arms.

Hip Isolations

In disco dancing, the hip performs earthy movements with a lot of power. As in the waist exercises, you should be relaxed with your feet planted into the floor as if they were glued to it. Your knees should be bent comfortably but not deeply, and you should really be able to feel the floor supporting your body.

Most of the hip motions below are based on the pushing movement that created the dance, The Bump. In pushing your hips, regardless of direction, try to imagine bouncing against a wall as your stopping point.

bumping to the right, and vice versa. Practice this first in each direction, and then alternate sides to the 32-count series described on page 25.

The Bump. Stand erect, and push your hip forcefully to the right, rebounding when you hit the imaginary wall. Repeat with the left side, and then practice in an alternating, left-right series. In this and the following hip exercises, keep your shoulders as steady as possible and focus all your attention on the hips.

Hip Rotation. As in the other rotations, the idea is to draw a circle in space, this time with the hips. To complete a smooth circle, picture yourself inside a cylinder, with your hips brushing its walls as you trace a circle. Practice this to a steady rhythm.

Forward Bump. Make the same motions as in the regular bump, but thrust your hip out to the front. To make this move more natural, place your right foot in front of the left when

Figure Eight Rotation. The figure eight is similar to the hip rotation, but you form a figure eight in space rather than a circle. Your spine should be at the center of the figure. Note that your knees *should* bend a little during this exercise. It will be difficult to follow through on the motion if your legs are stiff.

Knee Isolation

To isolate your knee, point your right toe and knee to the right side, at a comfortable distance from your left. Raise your heel, so that the weight of your body is on the ball of your foot. In this exercise, your foot will twist into the floor as if you are stomping out a cigarette. With heel raised, swing your knee—still bent—toward the front and then back to the side. You will be able to feel this action at your hip as well.

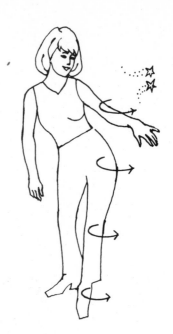

Progressive Rotation

This is a series of isolations that helps you get the feel of moving the whole right or left side of your body. In this case, you start with the foot and gradually work your way up to the shoulder and head, adding one rotating part to the next until your body is rotating. This requires a little more concentration than the individual isolations. To get the best results, think of your body as being anchored to the floor by the ball of your foot. As you proceed through the exercise, each of your joints, or rotation points—the ankle, the knee, the hip, the torso, the shoulder and the head—serves as a pivot point and controls the actual motions. Each time you add a new body part, you change the focus of your movement and let the preceding parts follow through and retain their action. As such, this is the culmination of all rotation. Once you can do this, you're on your way to the dance floor.

This four-part exercise should be completed all the way through for each side. With your feet parallel and slightly apart, raise your heel as in the knee isolation. Twist your foot to get the feel of the floor and to stabilize your body. Spread your toes a bit to get a better grip on the floor, pushing the ball of your foot into the floor. First, rotate your ankle by rubbing your toes against the floor, starting with the big toe and working to the small toe. To check yourself, look down at your foot; your ankle should be rotating in a clockwise circle. Now, continue the ankle rotation, but change your focus to the knee and rotate the knee with the ankle. Next, add the hip to the rotation. Finally, rotate the whole side; your head, shoulder and arm will be carried along with the motion. The whole side of your body should be carving out a circle at each pivot point to make the rotation smooth. Repeat all steps for the other side of the body.

Leg Isolations

Leg movements can swing, thrust, kick or unfold. Here are some basic exercises to work the legs and ankles. To increase your energy, try changing the music again, choosing an upbeat, swinging tune.

Forward and Backward Leg Thrust. The leg thrust is basically a smooth motion using the whole leg, with straight knees. Thrust your leg forward as if someone hit the back of your thigh, brushing the sole of the foot until it leaves the floor with toes pointed downward. Now, let your leg swing back so that the feet are parallel again. Your movement need not be too high. Notice that your ankle is stretched as you point your toe, and is flexed when you return to the feet-together stance. Try the same motion backward; remember to end with your toes pointed downward. To practice this, alternate forward and backward thrusts with the right and left legs, to eight beats as in the illustration.

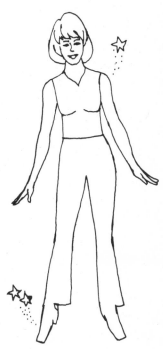

Side Leg Thrust. Keeping the knee forward, do the same movement as in the previous exercise, but thrust each leg out to the side, returning your feet to a parallel position each time.

Knee Bends. The knee bend, or plie, ties together everything accomplished so far. While it is not difficult to do, it is crucial to all dance. *The knee bend is the major link in good movement.* It gives fluidity to all dance, transforming a series of disjointed steps into a true dance.

Keep your feet and knees close together and bend from the knees, keeping heels on the floor and back straight. Imagine knocking on a door with both knees as they drop forward. Practice this in shallow bends and deep bends, eight fast bounces and a low squatting motion, down four counts and up four counts. If you feel a little soreness in the thighs and calves, shake your legs a little.

At this point, you should be ready to put together various movements that you have learned. Beginning with a slow and steady pace, start doing shallow knee bends to eight beats, and add one of the other, simple isolations. If you can do both at the same time, you can dance.

As an alternative, try the following sequence of thrusts and knee bends. It's fun to do, and involves real moving, so it should prove to you that you *can* dance, after all. Establish a steady beat in your mind. Thrust on count one and come together on "and," so that your rhythmic pattern is 1-and, 2-and, 3-and. Change to the other side and count again. Now thrust forward with your right leg four times. Then thrust the left foot forward four times. Then thrust your right leg to the side four times, and your left leg to the side four times. Next, thrust your right leg backward four times, and your left leg backward four times. Try repeating the pattern of thrusts on a series of two, and for a real challenge, repeat once in each direction. Practice the single-beat series until you feel comfortable with it— right leg forward, left leg forward; right leg to the side, left leg to the side; right leg backward, left leg backward.

This is where the fun begins. Practice the series of single thrusts with the supporting leg straight on count one and bending your knee when the foot comes back to the parallel position. This is a bouncy motion that is almost contagious. You'll find that your arms and hands have caught the fever in the middle of the exercise. Are you swinging your arms or snapping your fingers? Even if you believe you can't walk and chew gum at the same time, practice will make this exercise automatic, as you kick and bend.

For the final challenge, add a walking motion to the thrusts and bends. Dancing really is just an extension of walking, so don't be frightened away from this exercise. Merely perform the preceding steps, but move forward. Don't worry if your feet do not return exactly to the parallel position.

If you can't master these combinations at first, just turn back to the isolations and practice some more. If you have mastered the thrusts, bends and steps, try the following exercise, which combines various parts of the body. Start with knee bends, establishing a steady rhythm, and one at a time, add the shimmy, the pull back and the bump. When you've managed to do all at once, in harmony, you're dancing one of the simple disco styles. Now that you're really stepping, your next move is onto the dance floor.

4
DISCO FUNDAMENTALS:
Steps, Turns and Breaks

Now that you have learned to move every part of your body, through the isolations in Chapter 3, you are really ready to put it all together. This doesn't mean that you should plan on running right out to your local disco and mesmerizing the crowds with your own complex version of the Latin Hustle. You still have a few basics to learn before you can acquire the style that says "disco."

At this point you should begin to feel that rhythm is as familiar as an old friend. You may even find yourself wanting to move around at the most inconvenient times just because disco music is playing. It's probably not a great idea to give in to it and tango across the office floor or down the supermarket aisles. But, on the other hand, don't fight it. Once you have opened yourself up to the allure of a pleasing rhythm, you must remain open to it to develop an individual quality of movement on the dance floor.

The steps, turns and breaks in this chapter take the isolations one step further. While the isolations provided the very basics of all movement, the steps, turns and breaks apply those basics in the fundamental moves that form all disco dances. In fact, the steps, turns and breaks included will give you everything you need to know for old and new, individual and couple disco dances.

To better understand the process that can make you a good dancer, try to think of dancing as a language comparable to your native verbal or written language. Your potential to learn dance or language is practically infinite if you start from the beginning, and proceed one stage at a time.

If you have ever learned a foreign language, or if you can remember learning to read and write as a child, you will know that you must learn the alphabet before you can learn to spell, pronounce and use words. This is true in dance as well. You must learn the isolations before you can hope to make sense of the movements in this chapter. As such, the isolations are the *ABCs*, or *alphabet*, of dance. When you put together specific movements that you learned through the isolations you come up with steps, turns or breaks, which could be considered the *words* of the dance language. If it makes it any easier to understand, try thinking of the steps as nouns, and the turns and breaks as verbs. Once you have mastered them, so that you understand the use and expression of each, you can form dance sentences by combining steps, turns and breaks to make your own statement. Finally, when you have experimented and practiced creating these sentences, you can move on to whole paragraphs, or the disco dances themselves.

The most important thing to keep in mind with this analogy is that it is up to you to add your own personal touches to the general feeling expressed by the dance, whether it is a line or couple dance, a funky or sophisticated style. Although the basic movements are prescribed for the Hustle, the Bus Stop and others, the real dancing comes in with the accents you add. Think of the motions you add to these basic rules as adjectives and adverbs, to describe or embellish your dance paragraph.

The movements that actually distinguish the Hustle from the Swing of the New Yorker from the Bus Stop are only skeletons of paragraphs. Doing the Hustle steps by themselves without your own input would be akin to Shakespeare writing, "I don't like the sky," rather than, ". . . this most excellent canopy, the air, look you, this brave o'erhanging firmament, this majestical roof fretted with golden fire, why, it appears no other thing to me but a foul and pestilent congregation of vapours."

The following movements—or words—are divided into three basic categories—steps, turns and breaks. Don't try to skip the instructions for these and go straight to the dances. Done with practice and repetition, the steps, turns and breaks will help you learn the dances much faster, by making them a natural part of your movement pattern. The instructions for the disco dances in Chapter 5 will repeatedly refer to the material in this chapter. Rather than burden the reader with long, complex details on exactly how far to move the left foot while swinging the right arm, the dance steps are given as series of the steps, turns and breaks. So, it is important that you know how to use the appropriate "words" before you attempt a whole "paragraph."

Again, it helps to review how natural dance is to us. Historians think dance, or at least gestures, probably formed man's language. As such, dance is more natural to us than speaking or writing. Elementary level school teachers have even found that young students with the most highly developed coordination and physical skills learned their native verbal language more quickly and easily, especially in the initial concepts of alphabet recognition and imitation. Many teachers feel that the directional concepts involved in dance and all other movement are at the heart of this aptitude for language and reading. On the same note, music teachers have found that dancers learn to play an instrument more easily than non-dancers, perhaps because of their previous knowledge of rhythm and keeping time with their bodies.

Steps

A step is one of the most basic "words" in the dance language. Basically, a step is nothing more than the transference of weight from one side or foot to the other. Keep in mind that the human body is generally symmetrical, with identical left and right halves. Consequently, any move you make can be done with either side, or in either direction. In other words, you can step only with either the left foot or the right foot. If you feel like you have two left feet, just be thankful that you don't have four or eight feet to worry about. This is not as facetious as it sounds; it really helps in learning dances to remind yourself that no matter what the steps, you're only dealing with two legs, just as in walking. After all, dancing is just an extension of walking.

In fact, just about every movement involved in dance is based on direction or design in space, as in Chapter 3. All moves in this chapter are based on the creation of a design in space in a certain direction. Besides right and left movements, there are moves over and under, up and down, forward and backward. A good rule to remember when practicing a sequence of steps, turns and breaks is the old physics standby: for every action there is an equal and opposite reaction. The dance concept of fall and recover is based on the same principle. When you dip down, you must rise up. When you step left, you usually follow by stepping right.

Besides transferring your weight from one side to the other, a step is what makes it possible for us to cover ground. Without steps, all dance would be done in place, just as swimming without the armstrokes is merely treading water, and pedaling a bicycle without tires to grip the ground is just so much exercise.

Step. The basic step is nothing more than a walk, which can be done in any direction. Just to convince yourself it is that easy, try walking around in all directions, regardless of how silly it may look. Let yourself go and exaggerate or elaborate on the walk, moving the rest of your body with your legs and feet. Remember, it is the individual quality you interject that turns a militaristic walk into a dancing strut or slide, hop or swing.

Together. This is a very simple concept, but you have to understand it to follow the instructions for the paragraphs or dances. Basically, together means the same thing as recover. We use the word together because it helps dancers remember the concept. In general, when you see the word together, you should return to the starting position. For instance, if we say, "Step right, together, step left," the dancer brings his feet back to a parallel position, close together, after stepping to the right and before stepping to the left. In partner dances, together usually means that the couple comes back together in the starting position, after a break, a turn, or another type of movement.

Touch. The touch is almost as basic to dance as the step. In the touch, however, the ball of your foot touches the floor without transference of body weight. Again, really try to feel the floor as if it is part of your dance equipment, and simply press the ball of your foot, heel raised, into the floor, as if you were turning on the high beams of your auto headlights. Remember the importance of the stopping point: you can touch your foot at any spot within the outer circle your foot is capable of tracing in a rotation. To practice touches in the spots most often used in disco steps, touch your right foot directly forward, to the right side, directly backward and back together. Note that the design you form with your feet will be a triangle, and that your feet will alternate roles when you come back to the together position.

Did you think of touching one foot to the outside of the supporting foot? This is called a crossover touch: Cross one foot over and around the supporting leg and touch the floor; the motion will place one knee in front of the other.

These touches should definitely be done barefoot at first. Disco involves many influences from modern or jazz dance, which today is based on a love affair with the floor. Really get to know your floor. This is not tap dancing; dig in with the ball of your foot. Practice to four counts by touching in the series front, side, back, together.

Try this sequence for practice with touches and steps: Step with your right foot and cross your left foot front for the touch. Now step on the left and cross your right foot front for the touch. Step to the right and cross your left foot behind for the touch; then step to the left and cross the right behind for the touch. Now perform a side movement: Step right, then bring the left foot together with the right on a touch. To reverse, step left and bring your right foot back together on a touch.

Hop. This is simply a jump into the air on one foot. Don't get too carried away at first. Simply bounce moderately well off the floor on your right foot as if you were running in place on one foot. Try with the left foot.

Dig. The dig is done with the heel, and is used in funky and/or freestyle disco, rather than partner dances. Like the touch, this is not a tap. Dig your heel into the floor as if you were scuffing the heel of your shoe. Just bend your leg at the knee and dig into the floor with your heel. Notice that this is difficult to do backward, so don't bother with it. Practice this percussive move in any pattern of beats and at all points within the circle you can make with your knee.

Heel Click. This seasoned move has played a role in diverse folk dances through the ages. Today, it is used on the disco floor, mainly in freestyle and line dances. With your feet close together and parallel, lift your heels and click them together. In disco and other dances, this is usually done two clicks at a time. Practice pairs of clicks to varying tempos.

Step-touch. The step-touch is merely that: a step with one foot followed by a touch with the other. This is a specifically directional move; you can step-touch to the front, to the side, and to the back. Try various step-touches.

One important variation on the step-touch is the *touch-step,* which is somewhat the same, but both movements are done with the same foot. In other words, begin the series of moves with a touch and follow with a step on the same foot. This movement can be performed in any direction. Practice it while facing different directions.

Step-dig. Combine the step and the dig, as you did in the step-touch. Practice it in all directions, without bothering with backward digs, since these are hard to do and seldom used.

Ball-change. The ball-change is a common

disco movement, and is used in many partner dances. Basically, it is a touch-step combination, but you must touch with one foot and quickly step to the other. The movement is syncopated, quick and lively. As you practice, you may notice that several ball-changes in succession give a chugging train image.

This step can be done with the feet close together and parallel, or with one foot behind the other. If it helps, try saying to yourself while doing it, "ball-*change,* ball-*change,* ball-*change,*" or "touch-*step,* touch-*step,* touch-*step.*" The dancer's standard counting method would be, "and *one,* and *two,* and *three* ." Try not to dip backward on the ball-change when you practice it. To perfect it, imagine that you have a sore heel and cannot put it down on the floor, forcing you to limp. The weight then is transferred on the step, or change, portion.

Step-ball-change. Again, link a basic step with a ball-change. This is a syncopated series of three beats: *step,* ball-change, *step,* ball-change, *step,* ball-change or *step* and one, *step* and two, *step* and three. Try starting with a step on the right foot, which will give you the series right, left, right. Starting with the left foot, the steps will reverse to left, right, left. Remember, the weight is transferred on the step portion of the step-ball-change.

Kick-ball-change. The first thing to note about this move is that the kick is different from the leg thrusts described in Chapter 3. The kick is done with the bottom half of the leg, not with the whole leg. It is the type of kick you use when you kick a pebble or can along a sidewalk; the action is in the knee. In the kick-ball-change move, you will not be able to alternate legs, as in the step-ball-change, because the kick does not provide a true transference of weight. Kick front with the right foot, then do the ball-change from right foot to left. Repeat with the left foot kicking forward. The kick-ball-change is most often done to the front, but it can be done to the side as well. Don't try to do this one backward; it's difficult to do and rare on the dance floor.

Step-kick-ball-change. Put the step, the kick and the ball-change together. Step with the right foot, kick with the left, and ball-change (left-right). Notice that all of your weight is now on the right foot. Therefore, the only foot you can step on is the left, and the sequence reverses. Keep in mind that you transfer weight from one side to the other only on the step portion of this move.

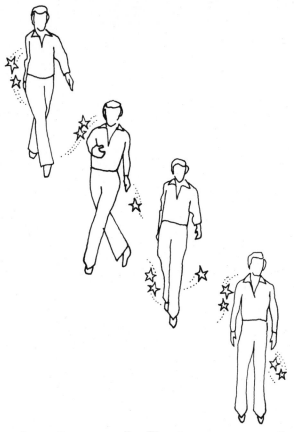

Jazz square walk. The jazz square walk is made up of four basic steps. Each step gets one count. Imagine a square on your floor and stand in the center of it. With the right foot, step to the upper left corner of the square. Now cross the left foot over to the upper right corner of the square. Bring the right foot back to the lower right corner and finsih with the left foot, stepping to the lower left corner to complete the square. Reverse the jazz square walk by starting the series with a left-foot step to the upper right corner, and crossing to the left front corner with the right foot, etc.

Grapevine. The grapevine will be familiar to

American square dancers and to those who know tap or soft-shoe dancing. It is also a well-used movement in disco line dances. The grapevine is a weaving, lateral movement done with the feet. Do the grapevine mainly on the balls of your feet; flat-footed steps make for a very heavy dance. Step right with the right foot, then behind with the left; step right with the right foot and cross in front with the left. You can do a grapevine as far as your room permits. End the pattern with a touch together. Try it to fast and slow beats, making a conscious effort to use the balls of your feet when extra speed is required.

Lunge. Starting with feet together, step either to the right, to the front or to the side, bending the supporting knee, and transferring the body weight on the bent leg. The other leg is extended straight. This could be described as a forward or side dip, very much like a fencing thrust executing the touche movement. You can recover from the fall by throwing the extended leg up to the bent leg, or vice versa.

Dip. The dip is a common move in the basic partner dances, and lends itself to all kinds of variety. Basically, the dip is a backward fall supported by your legs. Start by placing the ball of one foot, with heel raised, behind the other foot. Now, keeping your back straight, let your body weight carry you backward to a tilted position. In other words, try to imagine yourself bouncing backward to hit a slantboard. The dip should be a rocking motion, so bounce back to the upright position and do a dip to the other side. Keep in mind that when you place your right foot behind the left, you dip toward the left, and when you place your left foot behind the right, you dip toward the right.

Latin Basic

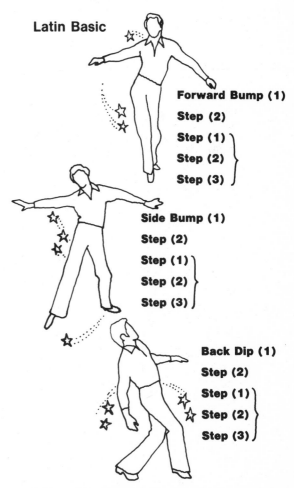

Forward Bump (1)

Step (2)

Step (1)

Step (2)

Step (3)

Side Bump (1)

Step (2)

Step (1)

Step (2)

Step (3)

Back Dip (1)

Step (2)

Step (1)

Step (2)

Step (3)

The Latin Basic. This is the cornerstone of

all Latin-flavor dances on the disco scene. It is really just a series of five steps. The secret ingredient here is the rhythm. The Latin Basic is two slow beats, followed by three fast. Sound familiar? It's the basic cha-cha step, so if you're familiar with that '50s dance, it might help to repeat to yourself: one, two, cha-cha-cha. We think, however, that it might be easier to do the Latin Basic while saying bump, step, step-step-step. This describes the movement and really does help you practice. Start by doing a forward bump with your right hip with a small step forward, then step in place on the left foot, and do three quick steps in place: right, left, right. The series can be reversed to begin with the left foot, of course. Keep in mind that the beats are quick, so the steps should be small ones, not leaping bounds. Also, remember that the hip action often makes the Latin dance. If you need to get the feel of this once more, refer back to the hip isolations in Chapter 3, and just add the steps. Besides the hip action, individualized and emotional flourishes are crucial to carrying off a Latin dance. On the first step of the Latin Basic, your whole body should come into play with the forward hip bump. And on the three quick steps at the end, don't just let your hands hang there. Experiment with the hand isolations you've learned. Practice this move to the front, the side and the back. Notice that when you do the series backward, the combination becomes dip, step, step-step-step.

Individual Turns

Turns are used in line dances, freestyle disco and couple dances. In all cases, the most important thing to remember is that all turns require you to make a complete revolution or rotation of the body. You must end a turn at the same point at which you started, facing in the same direction. The following turns are those used commonly by single dancers. They play a role in some of the established line dances, but can be used according to your creativity in freestyle dancing.

Pivot Turn. Everyone has done a turn like this at one time or another, but the trick is in making sure you do a complete revolution on the pivot. Imagine that there is a line drawn on the floor in front of and behind you, and stand in the middle of it. Starting with the right foot, take two steps forward on the line. Make a sharp right turn to face the opposite direction and repeat the sequence of steps and turn to face forward again. As you do a series of these, you'll begin to realize that the foot which does the first step stays basically on the same point on the line. This becomes your pivot point—hence the name, pivot turn.

Three-Point Turn. This turn is executed first on one side and then on the other. It is a three-step, lateral turn. Concentrate on direction to make a smooth circle. For this turn, imagine a line drawn on each side of you. Step right, then left, then right. These steps will change the direction you face. Face forward, then backward, then forward again on the line, always turning and progressing in the same direction. You should be making a complete revolution.

Chain Turn. This is really nothing more than a quick series of three-point turns, and should be practiced to a series of eight counts. Let the spirit take you on as many turns as you can fit in without crashing into a wall. You can do this quickly or slowly, but it is sort of an advanced step to do quickly without causing bodily damage to yourself and other hapless dancers nearby. Beware of dizziness on the chain turn.

Crossover Turn. This is a one-count, crossover-touch turn and is executed in one spot. With the supporting leg straight, cross your right foot over your left in a touch position, with knee bent. Now continue the move by transferring your weight and make a complete revolution to the left. This can also be reversed by crossing one leg behind the other and following that movement with a quick turn.

Swivel Turn. This is also a turn executed in one spot. A swivel turn is simply a complete turn on one foot. You can turn in either direction with either foot. What to do with the other leg: either lift it just a little and keep your heels close together or bend your knee more and pull your leg up so that the ankle is at the height of the other knee. Just be sure to keep your legs close together. Your arms should help you gain the momentum necessary to carry through the motion. Start with your arms open and gradually close them as you turn. For advanced practice, try to complete as many revolutions as you can before you lose momentum and have to put the other foot down.

The following pages of this chapter are devoted to the "words" you'll need to speak the language of disco partner dances. The couple dances bring a whole new concept into play. Armed with everything you have learned—from the isolations to the individual steps and turns—the prospect of stepping in time with a partner should be inspiring. If you thought that being able to dance by yourself, maintaining rhythm and developing a style, was fun, you will find partner dancing even more challenging—and more fun.

There is nothing like the thrill of dancing in harmony with another dancer. And if you really know the material in the preceding chapters, all you must remember to begin learning the partner dances is to relax. The new concept involved in dancing with a partner is that you must be able to feel where your partner is going and how he or she moves. And while you shouldn't hang like a limp rag from your partner's arms, neither should you stand rigidly at attention. Your muscles and nerves should be stimulated and ready for action—hopefully, as a result of doing the warm-up routine in Chapter 3. If you are nervous or tense, your own muscles will have a hard time receiving messages from your partner's muscles. You don't have to know your partner well to receive these messages; you just must be open to them. In a certain way, dancing with a partner is like riding a motorcycle, a surfboard or any other vehicle that requires balance—only much easier. On a motorcycle, you learn to shift your body weight gradually so that you and the bike lean together at the same time. Exactly how much weight you shift, and how fast, depends on the weight of the motorcycle and the degree of the turn you are making. After a trip or two around the dance floor with a particular partner, you will begin to feel the quality and style of your partner's movements. Then, you in turn will be able to respond, or lead, in kind.

While it is necessary for the man especially to give his partner extra support on some dance moves, partners should generally maintain a light contact between them. For basic movements, an extra-tight grip or clasp by one partner will only restrict the movements of the other. If you feel really hampered or weighted down by your partner while you dance, something is wrong. Once you've gotten the hang of it, dancing with a partner should provide additional excitement but the same freedom of movement that single dancing offers.

Before you try any of the turns or breaks used in partner dances, you must learn the various starting positions. While the individual steps, turns and dances focus on the feet and legs and leave the rest up to the dancer, the partner dances involve specific movements of the hands, arms and shoulders, etc. Note that the clasps and body positions change according to the dance being performed.

Couple Hand Positions

As in every other letter of the alphabet we've reviewed so far, the hand positons tend to come naturally after a while, but to know how to start, the following are some basics.

Vertical Clasp. This is the standard ballroom dance hand position. The man holds the woman's right hand in his left hand, palms together, fingers relaxed and hands pointing upward.

Swing Clasp. Start in the same position as for the vertical clasp, with both hands of each dancer clasped to the partner's hands, and extend arms out horizontally, relatively straight.

Latin Clasp. This clasp gives a lot more mobility,but has a variation for extra support on breaks. In this clasp, the man places his left thumb vertically in the woman's right palm and wraps the forefinger and middle finger around the back of her hand. For a stronger lead in breaks, the man presses the last two fingers of his left hand around his partner's wrist.

Curled Clasp. This is used mainly in turns and breaks. The woman turns her palm up and curls her fingers. The man clasps her fingers between thumb and the remaining fingers.

Couple Body Positions

The Standard. This is the common starting positon for most ballroom or social couple dances, past and present. The partners face each other but look over each other's shoulder. The man's right hand is placed below the woman's left shoulder blade, palm facing in. The woman's left hand rests lightly on her partner's right shoulder. With elbows bent, the man's left hand and the woman's right hand are clasped. The vertical clasp is used to start most dances.

Swing Position. Partners face each other again, but hold both arms out to the side, hands clasped in the swing clasp. The arms should be straight or bent slightly, held almost parallel to the floor.

Breaks

The following moves are for couples only. Breaks are moves whereby the partners separate momentarily during the dance, remaining connected at one point. Basically, the couple breaks from the basic body position used and opens up the stance.

Open Break. Starting in the standard posi-

tion, partners open their stance, the woman stepping to the right, the man to the left, breaking the hand clasp as well. Both partners should do a slight dip on the swing out. What opens does have to close in this case, so step back to the original position and break again. Practice.

Double Open Break. Repeat the same moves as in the open break, but break twice: open, close, open, close. Many disco dances call for the double open break.

Reverse Open Break. This is also a double break, but the partners move in the opposite direction on the second break. Do an open break (remember to dip) and close; now break to the other side: the woman steps and dips to the left and the man to the right. Essentially, the couple ends up facing one direction and then the other.

across the body so that the forearms are parallel. At the same time, the woman swings her right foot across her left, and the man swings his left foot over his right. The outside arms will swing out naturally; the foot pattern is step over, step back and together. Reverse the break by changing clasped hands as you cross over to the other side—step over, step back, and together.

Partner Turns

A partner dance would hardly be a partner dance—and never a disco dance—without turns. Again, every turn must make a complete revolution. With a partner, you have two options: one-hand turns or two-hand turns.

ONE-HAND TURNS

Arm Slide Break. This is an exciting move done often in disco. Start in the swing body and hand positions, but still facing each other, move to the side so that the woman's right side is adjacent to the man's right side. Simultaneously, both partners lift their arms up and over each other's head. The extended arms will be crossed as they are lifted between partners, and both will end up with hands clasped behind their necks. The extended arms then should be slid down the partner's arm to end by catching in a hand clasp.

Crossover Break. Start in the standard body position. Swing the clasped hands

Coil Turn. The dancers perform this turn with the linked arms outstretched. Holding the woman's left hand in his right, the man coils the woman into his right arm. She turns in to the left toward her partner, then uncoils to a straight-arm position again, as the man uncoils her. The woman is actually doing two three-point turns: one in and one out. This turn is reserved for the woman, but the man should guide her and help her follow through the action.

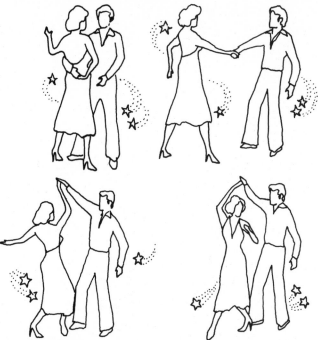

Whip Turn. This is similar to the coil turn but the couple starts in the standard body position. To start the turn, the man moves the clasped hands to the small of the woman's back, then switches hands so that his right hand is holding her right hand behind her back. He then uncoils the woman as she steps out with a right turn (a three-point turn). Follow through with a right turn under, or break hands and step together to resume the standard body position.

Right and Left Turn Under. This is a standard turn from the days of rock and roll, the jitterbug and other dances. Several turns can be done in succession; they can be done to the right or to the left. Basically, the partners raise the clasped hands and the man turns the woman under her right arm for a right turn and under her left arm for a left turn. The woman makes a complete circle while the couple holds hands loosely overhead for extra mobility. You can do the turn under with clasped left hands, right hands, or opposite hands, either to the right or to the left. Experiment with all the combinations, and spice it up with a deep knee bend on the turn. Remember, the man can turn under, too!

Open Break Turn. The starting position is similar to the open break stance, in which the partners are facing the same direction, standing side by side. Instead of holding hands, however, arms should be clasped around each other's waist. The woman then begins to step—with style—backward, while the man steps forward, so that the straight line between them is retained. Think of yourself as attached to the spokes of a turning wheel. Practice and reverse directions—clockwise or counterclockwise.

TWO-HAND TURNS

arms either to the right or to the left, stop with hands overhead. Rather than completing the turn, the man loops his arms over the woman's head, and around her waist, so that he is standing behind her. Unwrap and practice.

Wrap Turn. This is basically a two-handed turn under—either right or left—in which you stop halfway through the turn. Start in the swing position. With both partners raising their

Wringer Turn. This is the wrap turn completed. Just continue to swing the arms over, and turn all the way through.

Back-to-Back Turn. Start to do a wringer turn, but stop when partners are back to back. Keep your hands clasped. Both partners make a full clockwise spin on the floor, holding the back-to-back position. To return from the back-to-back position, complete a wringer turn to finish facing each other.

Straight Arm Pinwheel. To start, stand in the basic swing position, but raise your arms to shoulder level. Now step to the side so that right sides are adjacent. Your right arm will be held across your partner's chest and your left arm will have to flex to remain joined to your partner's. Remember, this is a two-hand turn. Now, partners simply walk forward in a clockwise direction, completing a full circle.

It is also important to practice the turn by changing the starting position so that your left sides are together and left arms are straight across your partner's chest. Practice this walking clockwise; both partners should be walking backward.

Reverse Straight Arm Pinwheel. This turn combines the forward and backward pinwheels described above. Assume the same starting position with right sides together. Take four steps forward in a clockwise circle. Now, in one move, make a quick switch to the left-side position while taking four steps backward; you should continue to move in a clockwise circle. Both hands of each partner remain joined throughout the turns, and partners should practice by switching positions every four counts.

Waist Pinwheel. Start with right sides together as above, but place your right arms around each other's waist. Your left arms will be extended outward to the side. As in the other pinwheels, execute the turn in a clockwise direction. For a variation, put your left sides together and rotate counter-clockwise.

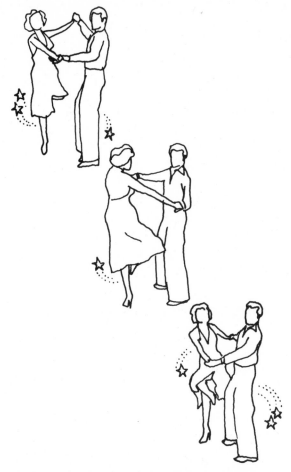

Swirl. Starting in the swing position, the man braces the woman's hands firmly with his own. Each swirl consists of a half-turn by the woman. The woman swings her right foot across the left, then the left across the right, lifting the leg up to touch ankle to knee, as in the individual swivel turn. Imagine that you are putting the right foot where the left foot used to be, and vice versa. In swirling, the woman describes a figure eight on the floor and through her body. The man in turn describes a figure eight with his torso as he guides his partner's movement firmly with his right hand.

Steparound Turn. This turn is exactly what it sounds like. Starting in the standard positon, the man steps backward as the woman steps around him in a circle pattern. The man initiates the movement by crossing his left foot back, behind his right heel in a touch position. As he leads the woman around his left side he makes a backward circle by stepping from left to right to left to right. At the same time, the woman continues her movement by walking around him in a left-right-left-right pattern, finishing in the closed position. The turn will have more style if the woman leans slightly backward as she steps around her partner.

Spot Turn. This is a closed-position turn in which the partners rotate in place, or on one spot. It is most fun when executed as a four-step turn. Starting in the standard position, the man begins by placing his right foot to the inside of the woman's right foot, locking the sides of the knees together. Stepping naturally on the left foot, the partners maintain a closed body position and alternate left and right steps as they rotate together in a clockwise direction. To maintain balance, the man should hold the woman firmly with his right hand while she presses her left hand against his right shoulder blade. This is an exciting turn and can really gain momentum. Once you have mastered it, you may even try to progress across the floor with it.

If the previous material seems like a lot to learn without ever finding out how to do the Hustle, don't be discouraged. When you truly know the "words" in this chapter, you have everything you need to dance a whole paragraph. Learning the dances that follow in Chapter 5 will merely be a matter of memorizing a couple of sentences, or sequences of steps, breaks and turns.

5
STEPPING OUT:
Freestyle,
Line
and Couple Dances

On the following pages are the final keys you need to open the door to the world of disco. If you have warmed up with the isolations and practiced the whole spectrum of steps, turns and breaks, you will find the dance instructions in this chapter easy to follow. With practice, you should be able to glide through every dance described, adding your own style as you go along.

The dances we cover here should be considered the base, or foundation, of your disco repertoire. We chose the dances included for their longevity and popularity on the disco scene, and because they lend themselves to extensive modification. Build on them with variations of your own creation. The steps, turns and breaks used in each dance can be combined in any of at least a hundred ways.

Disco has been called an erotic cultural force, a description which is borne out by the "anything goes" attitude of today's dancers. Everyone wants to be a star, and to be a star among millions, you really have to stand out. So let yourself go—the natural expression of disco dancing allows your body movements to beat like the rhythm of a drum speaking a non-verbal language. There is no way to express the exhilaration of dancing in words, and unless you join the crowd, you will find it difficult to understand that language.

The disco look comes from a true melting pot of dance heritage. The group or line dances, along with freestyle disco, recall the rock and roll dances of the 1960s, and can be traced back even farther to the old national folk dances. The couple dances come from steps popularized during many dance eras. You'll catch hints of the jitterbug and the Charleston, the cha-cha and the tango and many others in today's dances.

With regular repetition and conscientious effort, you can experience body awareness and that source of inner energy that may have been buried for years. Disco dancing, like athletics, can give you a unique sense of well-being and confidence as you develop your own style on the dance floor. In fact, the disco fever can alter your entire lifestyle, bringing new excitement into your life, and giving you a new outlook on your surroundings. So why wait? Warm up, tune in...and step out!

Line-Freestyle Dances

The line dances that follow are energetic and really exciting when done with a large group. Even if you don't anticipate being able to get together a lot of dancers, learning the line dances will give you all the basic foot movements you need for the partner dances. The line dances also can be adapted as you choose for freestyle dancing. With a little extra thought and work, you can adapt the line dances for couples.

In all line or freestyle dances, what you do with each and every part of your body is entirely up to you. So warm up with the isolations and prepare to move. Try to visualize the music's rhythm emanating from your midsection and radiating out to your fingertips and toes, forcing every muscle to join in. Don't worry if you actually begin to sweat when you practice the dances—it just means you've caught the fever. Above all, don't be impatient. If you have trouble with a particular dance, refer back to the steps, turns and breaks in Chapter 4. If your problem seems to go deeper, return to Chapter 3 and practice the isolations.

Most of the line dances are based on geometrical figures drawn in space and on the floor by the group as a whole and by the individual dancers. The foot patterns of the individual dancers trace various squares, circles and triangles on the floor, while the body focus or the position of the whole group usually defines a square or a set of parallel lines. In other words, the dancers usually start out in a line, side by side, or in several lines, and as they proceed through the dance, they all change direction simultaneously. First they all face forward, then continue to turn to the side, or backward, as they repeat the entire sequence in the new direction.

Each whole dance or paragraph can be broken down into counts or beats, with a movement on each count. Thus, if the dance is an eight-count dance, it means that the series of eight movements is performed—usually on eight beats—until the music stops or the dancers cannot lift another foot. Besides actually counting out the beats to yourself, you can follow a few other rules to help in practice sessions. The first is that when you are in doubt, you should use the right foot, or arm, or whatever part is called for, first. It is better to do that and risk missing a step than to just stand there and gape while you try to remember which foot comes next. With practice, it'll come to you naturally. It also helps to speak the words of each step as you execute them: step-touch, step, step, etc. Finally, don't try to do too much too soon. Start out taking small steps, and dancing to a slow beat. As you feel comfortable with each series of movements, you can increase the tempo and embellishments.

NEW YORKER

The New Yorker. The New Yorker is a 20-count dance that is easiest to learn in four sections—one section of eight counts, and three sections of four counts each. Keep in mind that every section begins with the right foot. The four sections consist of steps, touches, dips and a grapevine.

I.   Start with your feet together and with the right foot, touch forward, together, forward, together (1,2,3,4). With the right foot again, touch front, side, back, together (the triangle foot pattern; 5,6,7,8).

II.   Repeat just the triangle touch pattern as above, with the left foot this time (1,2,3,4).

III.   The third part is a dip left (right foot back), together, dip right, together (1,2,3,4).

IV.   This final section is a little trickier. It's a basic grapevine, starting with the right foot again, but with a half-turn to the right on the last beat (1,2,3,4). With the half-turn, you will end up feet together, facing in the direction opposite from the one you started in.

Repeat all four sections—another 20 counts—to complete the New Yorker.

I

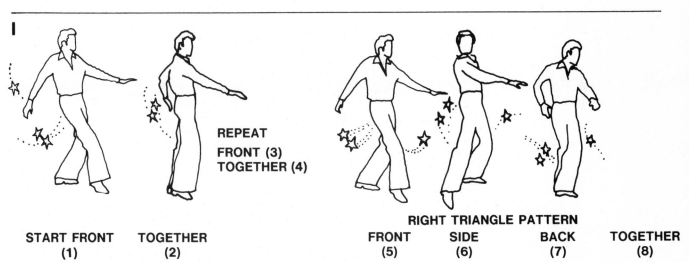

REPEAT
FRONT (3)
TOGETHER (4)

START FRONT   TOGETHER
(1)   (2)

RIGHT TRIANGLE PATTERN

FRONT   SIDE   BACK   TOGETHER
(5)   (6)   (7)   (8)

II

LEFT TRIANGLE PATTERN   TOGETHER
(1,2,3)   (4)

III

DIP   TOGETHER   DIP   TOGETHER
LEFT   RIGHT
(5)   (6)   (7)   (8)

IV

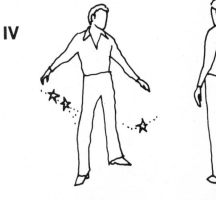

GRAPEVINE   TOGETHER
(1,2,3)   (4)

NEW YORKER

BUS STOP

BUS STOP

Bus Stop. In this line dance, each participant completes the whole dance facing in each of the four directions. The dance is a 40-count dance—160 counts if you count the fourfold repetition. *At the end of each series, the dancers turn to the left* (start forward, face left, face backward, face right). The Bus Stop is divided into five sections of eight counts each.

I. Start with a simultaneous kick forward with the right foot and a clap of the hands (1). Next, take three steps backward—right, left, right (2,3,4)—a touch together (5), and three steps forward: left, right, left (6,7,8).

II. The second section is an exact repeat of the first: kick & clap, step, step, step, touch, step, step, step-a total of eight more counts.

III. This is a grapevine step done both to the right and to the left. Starting with the right foot, step side, back, side, touch together (1,2,3,4). Reverse, starting with the left foot (5,6,7,8).

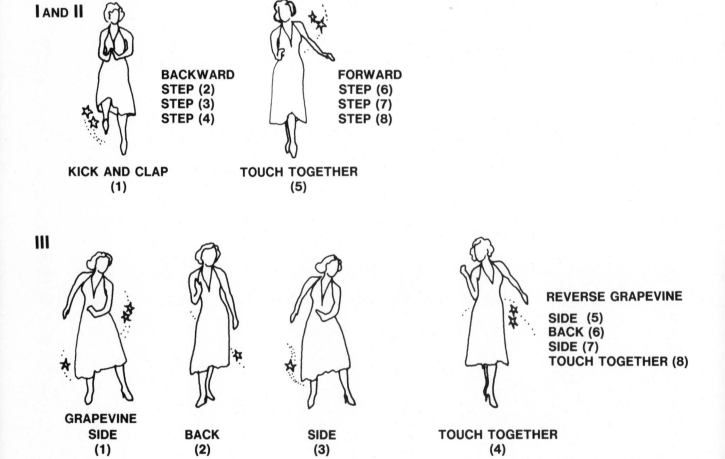

I AND II

BACKWARD
STEP (2)
STEP (3)
STEP (4)

FORWARD
STEP (6)
STEP (7)
STEP (8)

KICK AND CLAP
(1)

TOUCH TOGETHER
(5)

III

GRAPEVINE
SIDE
(1)

BACK
(2)

SIDE
(3)

TOUCH TOGETHER
(4)

REVERSE GRAPEVINE

SIDE (5)
BACK (6)
SIDE (7)
TOUCH TOGETHER (8)

IV. The fourth section is steps, touches and heel clicks. Starting with the right foot step right, touch together, step left, touch together (1,2,3,4). Follow with two heel clicks (5,6), a right foot touch forward and a right foot touch backward (7,8).

V. This final section is all touches, each done with the right foot. Touch front twice (1,2) and touch back twice (3,4). Touch front, touch back (5,6), touch together (7) and turn left on the final count (8).

Start the whole thing from the top and do the Bus Stop sequence to each of the four directions to complete the dance.

IV

| STEP SIDE (1) | TOUCH TOGETHER (2) | STEP SIDE (3) | TOUCH TOGETHER (4) | HEEL CLICK (5) |

| HEEL CLICK (6) | TOUCH FORWARD (7) | TOUCH BACK (8) |

V

| TOUCH FRONT (1) | TOUCH FRONT (2) | TOUCH BACK (3) | TOUCH BACK (4) | TOUCH FRONT (5) |

| TOUCH BACK (6) | TOUCH TOGETHER (7) | TURN (8) |

L.A. LOCK

L.A. Lock. A lock is a freestyle dance that signifies a style rather than a particular series of rhythmic steps. A lock is the most energetic, individualistic and eccentric of all disco dances, and some dancers feel it is the most difficult to perform as well. Locks are quite popular on the West Coast today and fall into the disco category Californians call punk. In other regions, however, you might hear the same type of dance called funky.

In order to achieve the total look, many lockers wear a particular style of dress that emphasizes their preference in dance styles and is compatible with the gymnastic moves of the lock. Although other types of clothes can be worn to do a lock, one example of the lock outfit might include striped T-shirt and socks, knickers or baggy pants, wide suspenders, vests, oxfords and puppy tails or caps.

Locking is a dance term that means just what it says. The dancer strikes an eccentric or angular pose and locks position for one or two counts, usually followed by a series of quick, sharp and abrupt movements. Double-takes at your partner or the audience on the other hand are called fast locks. Other unusual dramatics used in the lock might include gymnastic tricks such as round-offs and jumping to a split. These, however, are extreme forms of locking; many of the isolations in Chapter 3 actually are lock basics used frequently in disco. Again, you just assume a pose and lock the muscles into position. Here is an easy-to-follow lock dance.

I. The first section is eight counts. Start by facing front; you will be doing four steps foward starting with the right foot. Leading with the heel, step forward with the right foot (1). Then bend the supporting knee, press

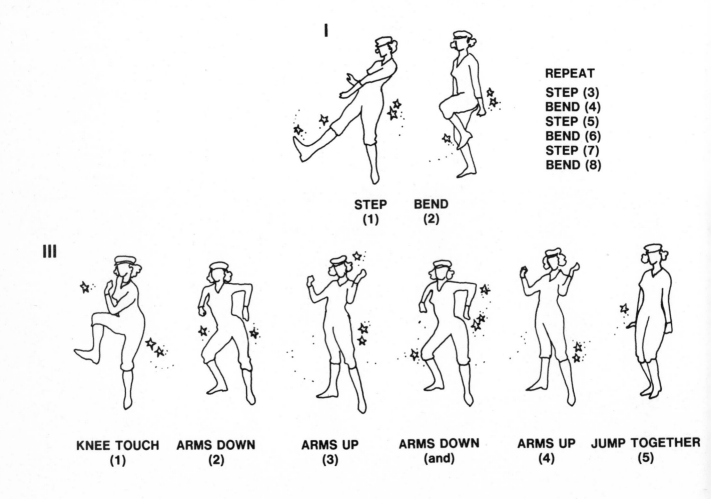

I

REPEAT
STEP (3)
BEND (4)
STEP (5)
BEND (6)
STEP (7)
BEND (8)

STEP   BEND
(1)   (2)

III

KNEE TOUCH   ARMS DOWN   ARMS UP   ARMS DOWN   ARMS UP   JUMP TOGETHER
(1)   (2)   (3)   (and)   (4)   (5)

both shoulders down and do a chin thrust as you raise your left knee waist level. (2) Repeat all the movements on the next three steps forward—left foot, right foot, left foot—(3,4,5,6,7,8).

II. The second section is knee bends (plies) and forearm locks in four counts with one movement on each count (1,2,3,4). First, jump to an open stance (a jump is just a two-footed hop), ending in a knee bend and doing an alternating forearm swing once, right arm going up, left arm down (1). Then straighten and lock your knees as both arms swing up in a forearm swing (2). Do a knee bend and another alternating forearm swing, left arm up and right arm down (3). Next, jump to bring feet together (4). Repeat these movements on 5,6,7,8.

III. The section is a full eight counts (1,2,3 and, 4,5,6 and, 7-and, 8, and). Raise your

right knee and touch it with your left elbow as you contract the torso (1). Then step the right foot to the side in an open stance with a knee bend and do a forearm swing—downward, this time using both arms. (2). Straighten your knees while doing forearm swings up. (3) Bend knees as arms swing down (and), straighten knees as arms swing up again. (4). Jump together dropping arms to your side. (5). Do a deep knee bend and slap the floor with both hands. (6). Jump upright (and). Now kick the right foot forward as you take an exaggerated step forward, leading with the heel (7-and). Note that this is like the movement known as "truckin'" during the 1960s. Now draw the left foot up to the right and together. (8). Finally, jump and turn to the left (a quarter-turn) to finish the lock dance (and). You can repeat the series as many times as you wish.

II

REPEAT
RIGHT ARM UP (5)
BOTH ARMS UP (6)
LEFT ARM UP (7)
JUMP TOGETHER (8)

RIGHT ARM UP (1)   **BOTH ARMS UP (2)**   **LEFT ARM UP (3)**   **JUMP TOGETHER (4)**

SLAP FLOOR (6)   **JUMP TOGETHER (and)**   **HEEL STEP (7 and)**   **STEP TOGETHER (8)**   **JUMP TURN (and)**

L.A. LOCK

NEW YORK HUSTLE

Couple Dances

To start out on the right foot, there are a few basic rules for most couple dances. Generally, the woman starts the dance with her right foot, the man with his left. Also, remember that the man initiates each move. As mentioned in

N.Y. HUSTLE

New York Hustle. The New York Hustle is probably one of the most popular of the disco partner dances. The basic rhythm pattern is in four counts and involves nothing more than steps and touches. The flourishes of turns and breaks make the New York Hustle basic look exciting. Style and dramatics are up to you and your partner. Listed below is a complete New York Hustle.

Start in the standard body position with the vertical hand clasp. The basic hustle is step side, touch together, step other side, touch together. Try to maintain that series of foot movements as you execute the breaks and turns in the dance, too. The dance described below is a total of 32 counts, and is divided into four sections.

I.   Both partners step side, touch together, step other side, touch together (1,2,3,4)—the woman beginning with the right foot, the man with the left. Repeat the basic hustle (5,6,7,8).

Chapter 4, the most important thing is communicating with your partner. The look in the eyes and the facial expression are just as important to the dance as the steps, turns and breaks. Think style, and assume the personality of each dance.

II.   First do an open break (1,2) and return (3,4). Then, facing each other again, do the basic hustle as in section one (5,6,7,8).

III.   Then, do a double open break (1,2,3,4,5,6,7,8).

IV.   The fourth section calls for a right turn under by the woman (1,2,3,4). Note that only two hands will be connected after the double open break; do the turn with those hands and arms. Next, do a basic hustle facing each other (5,6,7,8).

Once you've mastered the above 32 counts, try adopting either of the following variations. In the first variation, repeat the entire series of steps above, but replace the woman's right turn under with a left turn under by the man. Again, use the hands that are already clasped. A second variation calls for both partners to turn in the fourth section of the dance. At the same time, the man does a left turn under while the woman does a right turn under.

I

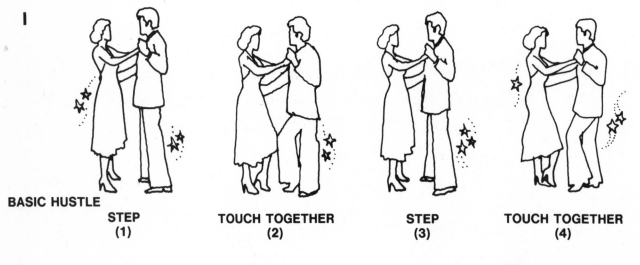

BASIC HUSTLE

| STEP (1) | TOUCH TOGETHER (2) | STEP (3) | TOUCH TOGETHER (4) |

REPEAT BASIC HUSTLE

STEP (5)
TOUCH TOGETHER (6)
STEP (7)
TOUCH TOGETHER (8)

II

REPEAT BASIC HUSTLE

STEP (5)
TOUCH TOGETHER (6)
STEP (7)
TOUCH TOGETHER (8)

STEP TOUCH STEP TOUCH
(1) (2) (3) (4)

III

REPEAT OPEN BREAK

STEP (5)
TOUCH (6)
STEP (7)
TOUCH (8)

OPEN BREAK   RETURN
STEP TOUCH   STEP TOUCH
(1) (2)   (3) (4)

IV

REPEAT BASIC HUSTLE

STEP (5)
TOUCH TOGETHER (6)
STEP (7)
TOUCH TOGETHER (8)

RIGHT TURN UNDER
(1,2,3,4)

CONTINENTAL HUSTLE

Continental Hustle. This is a popular modification of the basic New York Hustle, but is based on six rather than four counts. The Continental Hustle is just the New York Hustle plus two steps forward: step, touch, step, touch, step, step together (1,2,3,4,5,6). The last two steps can be done backward for variety. This is a six-section dance with a total of 36 counts. Continue doing the basic foot pattern of the Continental Hustle as you execute the breaks and turns.

I.   Starting in the swing position, the woman starts the first section to the right, the man to the left. Each partner does the basic hustle—step, touch, step, touch (1,2,3,4). Then the woman takes two steps backward as the man takes two steps forward (5,6). Remember that the second step is a step together.

II.   The second section is a repeat of the basic hustle (1,2,3,4), but the woman then takes two steps forward as the man takes two

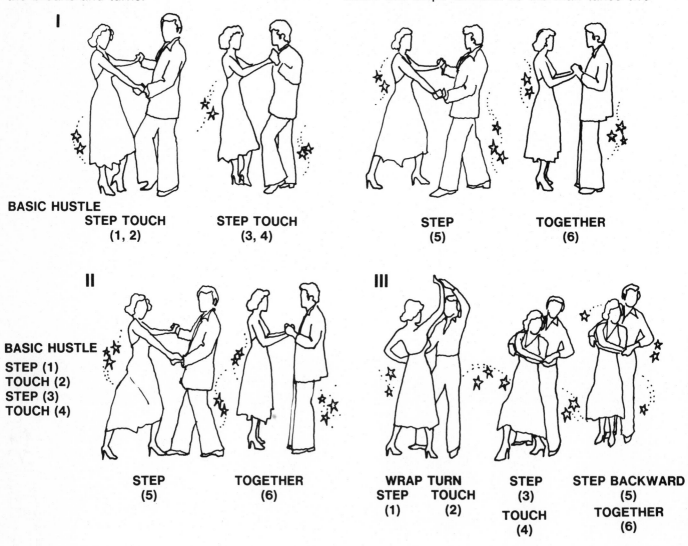

I

BASIC HUSTLE
    STEP TOUCH   **STEP TOUCH**   **STEP**   **TOGETHER**
      (1, 2)   **(3, 4)**   **(5)**   **(6)**

II

BASIC HUSTLE
STEP (1)
TOUCH (2)
STEP (3)
TOUCH (4)

         STEP   **TOGETHER**
          (5)   **(6)**

III

WRAP TURN   **STEP**   **STEP BACKWARD**
STEP   TOUCH   **(3)**   **(5)**
(1)   (2)   **TOUCH**   **TOGETHER**
                (4)   **(6)**

steps backward (5,6). Again, both partners finish with feet together.

III. In the third part, the couple does a wrap turn to the right on four counts (1,2,3,4). Maintaining the wrapped position, both partners step backward and together (5,6).

IV. Still in the wrapped position, the partners again do the Continental basic for the fourth part: both partners starting on the right foot, do the hustle basic (1,2,3,4), followed by

a step forward, by both partners (5,6).

V. Part five calls for another Continental basic in the wrapped position, both partners stepping right first, and finishing with both partners taking a step backward and a step together (1,2,3,4,5,6).

VI. The final section starts with the partners unwrapping from the original turn (1,2,3,4). Finally, the woman takes two steps forward as the man takes two steps backward (5,6).

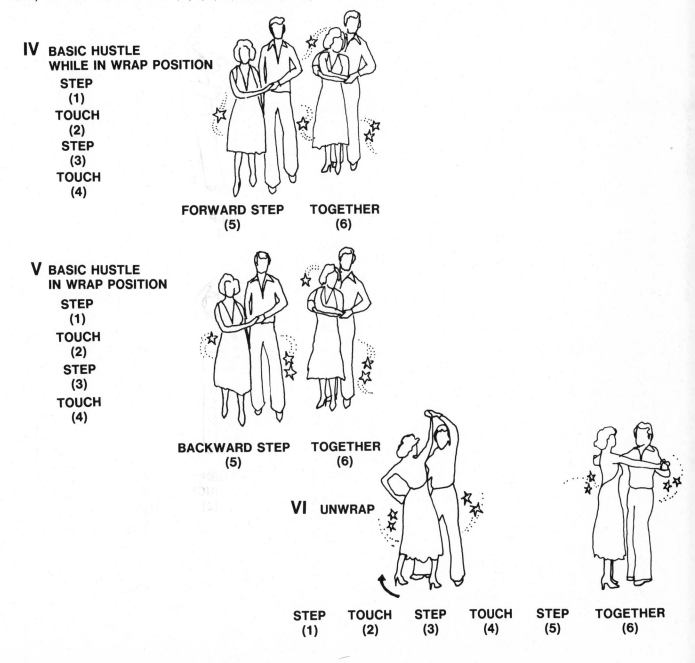

IV BASIC HUSTLE
WHILE IN WRAP POSITION
STEP
(1)
TOUCH
(2)
STEP
(3)
TOUCH
(4)

FORWARD STEP (5)   TOGETHER (6)

V BASIC HUSTLE
IN WRAP POSITION
STEP
(1)
TOUCH
(2)
STEP
(3)
TOUCH
(4)

BACKWARD STEP (5)   TOGETHER (6)

VI UNWRAP

STEP (1)   TOUCH (2)   STEP (3)   TOUCH (4)   STEP (5)   TOGETHER (6)

CONTINENTAL HUSTLE

LATIN HUSTLE

LATIN HUSTLE

Latin Hustle. The Latin Hustle is also a six-count dance. The basic movements involved are steps, touches, and ball-changes. The basic pattern is touch, step, ball-change, step, step, step (1,2,3-and,4,5,6). The woman begins the dance with her right foot, the man with his left. Note that the initial touch, step, can be done in either of two ways: touch to the side and step together; or touch together and step to the side.

This is a sophisticated and smooth dance and should be treated that way. Do a slight dip on the ball-change, and break open at the same time. Come back together as you take three steps forward. If you're confused about which foot to use at which point in the dance, try following this order if you're a woman (the opposite if you're a man): right, right, left-right, left, right, left. Here is a Latin Hustle that will wow the crowds at your local disco. It's in four parts, or 24 counts all together.

I.   Start in the standard position. Do the Latin Hustle basic as described, finishing in

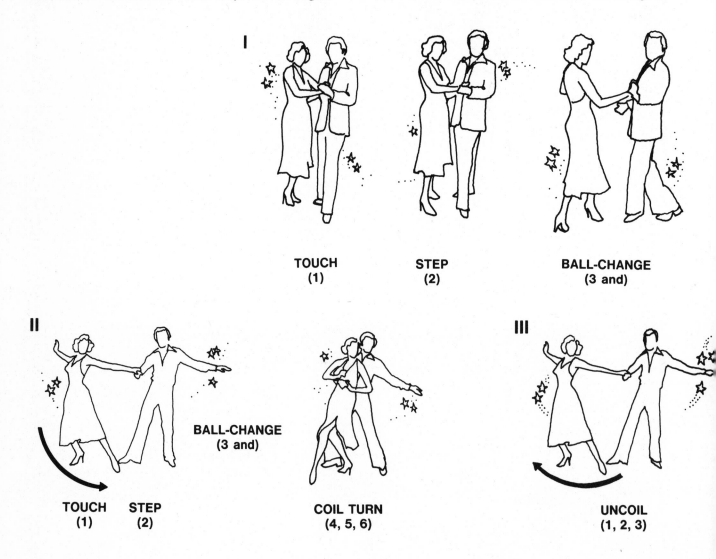

I

TOUCH
(1)

STEP
(2)

BALL-CHANGE
(3 and)

II

BALL-CHANGE
(3 and)

TOUCH   **STEP**
(1)   **(2)**

COIL TURN
(4, 5, 6)

III

UNCOIL
(1, 2, 3)

the swing position (1,2,3-and,4,5,6).

II.   Starting in the swing position repeat the Latin Hustle basic while executing an open break. Partners should be all the way apart on the ball-change (1,2,3-and). Then, the woman does a coil turn—a three-point turn left on the last three steps of the Latin Hustle basic (4,5,6).

III.   To start the third section, the woman uncoils out—another three-point turn right—(1,2,3), stepping right, left, right and finishes the section with a right turn under (4,5,6),

stepping left, right, left.

IV.   On the last section, the partners do the first part of the Latin Hustle basic while still apart (1,2,3-and), and then return to the standard body position on the last three steps (4,5,6).

When you're just beginning to learn the Latin Hustle described above, you might find it difficult to do one section after another smoothly. To practice, and on the dance floor, insert a few basic hustle steps between sections to collect your thoughts.

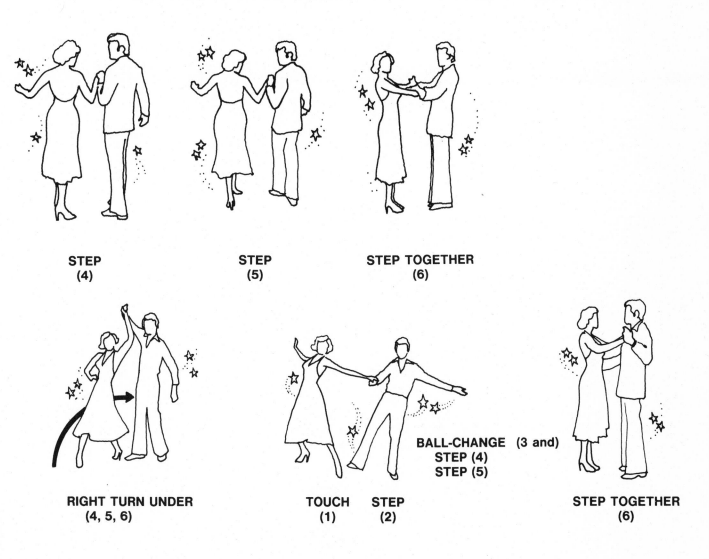

| STEP | STEP | STEP TOGETHER |
| (4) | (5) | (6) |

| RIGHT TURN UNDER | TOUCH   STEP | BALL-CHANGE (3 and) | STEP TOGETHER |
| (4, 5, 6) | (1)   (2) | STEP (4) / STEP (5) | (6) |

LATIN HUSTLE PLUS

Latin Hustle Plus. This is the Latin Hustle with a kick thrown in to make it an eight-beat dance in six counts. Follow this series: touch, step, ball-change, kick-step, step, step (1,2,3-and,4-and,5,6,). The kick should be small, since a quick step follows (4-and). The feeling should be smooth, and the couple should break open at the ball-change, as in the Latin Hustle, closing again after the final two steps which would be count one of the new phrase. Start the Latin Hustle Plus in the swing posi-

tion (one section has 12 counts; the rest have six each).

I.   Execute a crossover break, the woman crossing her right foot over, the man his left (1,2,3). Then, both partners do a crossover break to the other side (4,5,6).

II.   Execute a wringer turn, stopping the turn in the back-to-back position (1,2,3). Then, do a complete back-to-back turn (4,5,6,1,2,3). Now, finish the wringer turn to end face to face (4,5,6).

I

CROSSOVER BREAK
(1, 2, 3)

REVERSE
(4, 5, 6)

II

WRINGER
(1)

TURN
(2, 3)

BACK TO BACK TURN
(4, 5, 6,   1, 2, 3)

COMPLETE WRINGER TURN
(4, 5, 6)

III. The third section is just a Latin Hustle Plus basic (1,2,3-and,4-and,5,6).

IV. Now do a spot turn either in place or travelling across the floor (1,2,3,4,5,6).

V. The final section is another Latin Hustle Plus basic (1,2,3-and,4-and,5,6).

An interesting variation can be used by altering the first section of the dance. Rather than the crossover break, the woman executes a swirl turn, crossing with the right foot (1,2,3), then the left (4,5,6).

III LATIN HUSTLE PLUS BASIC

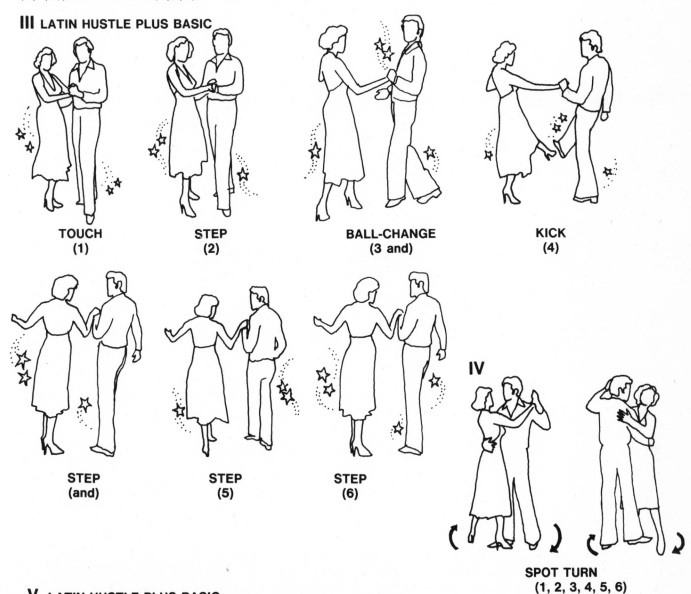

TOUCH (1)	STEP (2)	BALL-CHANGE (3 and)	KICK (4)

STEP (and)	STEP (5)	STEP (6)	**IV**

SPOT TURN
(1, 2, 3, 4, 5, 6)

V LATIN HUSTLE PLUS BASIC
REPEAT SECTION III
TOUCH, STEP, BALL-CHANGE, KICK, STEP, STEP, STEP
(1, 2, 3-and, 4-and, 5, 6)

LATIN HUSTLE PLUS

TANGO HUSTLE

TANGO HUSTLE

Tango Hustle. The Tango Hustle is the modern version of the Rudolf Valentino Special, and really is the epitome of the Hustle. The classic touches are retained, giving the dance a romantic and dramatic flavor. This is a real eye-catcher when done well, and gives the dancers a chance to cast meaningful glances at each other as they glide and dip smoothly across the floor. As it was in the 1920s, the Tango Hustle of today is quite sophisticated. The dancers' attire will contribute much to this dance's effect; blue jeans just won't give the same feeling as well fitted slacks for the man and a slinky dress for the woman.

The Tango Hustle is a 16-count dance split into two sections of eight counts each. Start in the standard position but lower the clasped arms and hold them out straight; now both partners turn to face the direction of those arms (right for the woman, left for the man).

I.   For the first section, the couple takes four steps forward, the woman starting on the

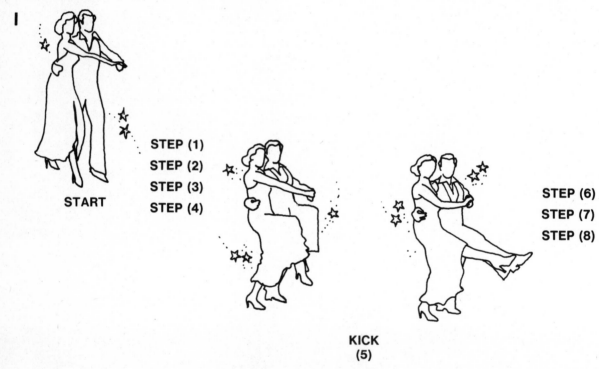

STEP (1)
STEP (2)
STEP (3)
STEP (4)

START

**KICK
(5)**

STEP (6)
STEP (7)
STEP (8)

right foot while the man starts on the left: step, step, step, step (1,2,3,4). The next series is a kick, two steps and a touch: for the woman, kick right, step right, step left, touch right together (5,6,7,8). The man reverses the foot sequence.

II.   Begin with a forward lunge (1,2,3). Come together again by drawing the bent legs back to the extended legs (4). Now do a steparound turn, the woman stepping around to the left (5,6,7,8).

For an interesting variation on section two, replace the steparound turn with an open break turn done clockwise and holding each other's waist.

II

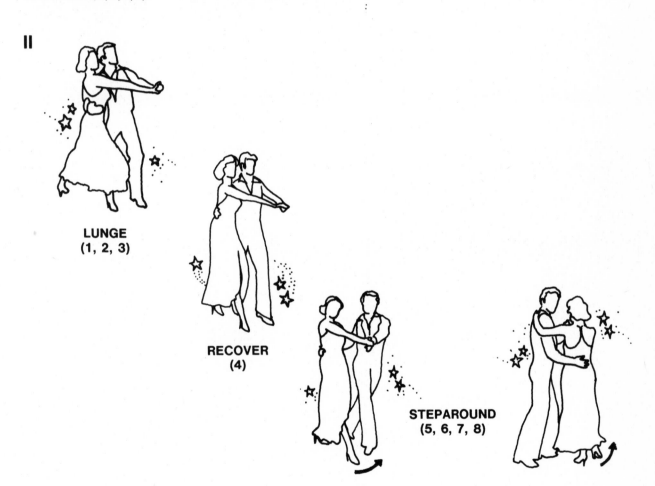

LUNGE
(1, 2, 3)

RECOVER
(4)

STEPAROUND
(5, 6, 7, 8)

SWING

Swing. Basically a revival of the 1927 Lindy Hop and the jitterbug of the '40s, the swing is a six-count dance. Starting with the right foot for the woman, the left foot for the man, the basic swing is: step, ball-change, step, ball-change, dip, step (1,and-2,3,and-4,5,6). Note that the dip is done with the right foot back for the woman, the left foot back for the man. On the dip, the couple does an open break and returns to the swing position to repeat the basic pattern. The following swing is divided into four sections. Start in the swing position.

I.   The first section is a basic swing step (1,and-2,3,and-4,5,6).

II.   Change your focal point to a different direction and do another basic swing step (1,and-2,3, and-4,5,6).

III.   The third section is a swivel turn and swing. The man releases the clasped hands as the woman executes a step right to a swivel

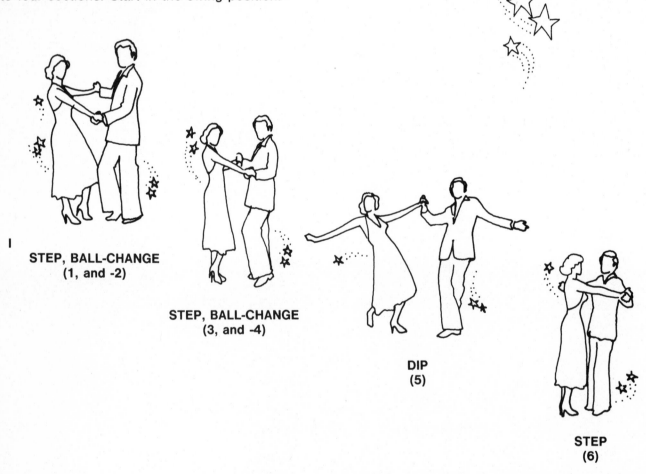

I

STEP, BALL-CHANGE
(1, and -2)

STEP, BALL-CHANGE
(3, and -4)

DIP
(5)

STEP
(6)

II

REPEAT
SECTION I IN A NEW DIRECTION

turn right; the man does a step left and ball-change (1,and-2). Then the woman does a step left and a ball-change, while the man does a step right and a swivel turn right (3,and-4). Finally, the partners join hands and do a dip followed by a step (5,6).

IV. Complete the swing by doing a basic swing step (1,and-2,3,and-4,5,6).

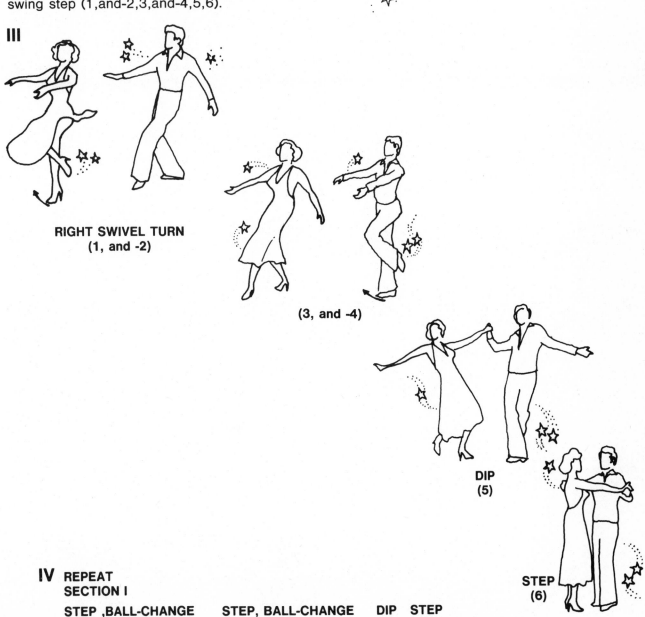

III

RIGHT SWIVEL TURN
(1, and -2)

(3, and -4)

DIP
(5)

STEP
(6)

IV REPEAT
SECTION I

STEP ,BALL-CHANGE	STEP, BALL-CHANGE	DIP	STEP
(1, and -2)	(3, and -4)	(5)	(6)

SWING

LOVER SWING

THE LOVER SWING

The Lover Swing. This is an intimate sort of swing in four sections. Rather than the swing position, however, start by facing each other and holding hands with wrists crossed.

I. Do the basic swing steps (1,and-2,3,and-4,5,6). While executing the lover arm movements: first draw the arms up overhead,

then smoothly uncross wrists and place hands lightly on partner's shoulders. Then, for the arm slide, draw your hands softly down the length of your partner's arms, and catch hands.

II. Now your hands are in the basic swing position. Do the basic swing step, but do not

I STEP ,BALL-CHANGE   STEP, BALL-CHANGE   DIP   STEP
   (1, and -2)   (3, and -4)   (5)   (6)

II STEP, BALL-CHANGE   STEP, BALL-CHANGE   DIP   STEP
   (1, and -2)   (3, and -4)   (5)   (6)

break hands on the dip step, as in the basic swing (1,and-2,3,and-4,5,6).

III. Do a whip turn, with the woman finishing the turn by doing a right turn under the man's right arm (1,2,3,4,5,6,).

IV. Repeat the basic swing step (1,and-2,3,and-4,5,6).

III

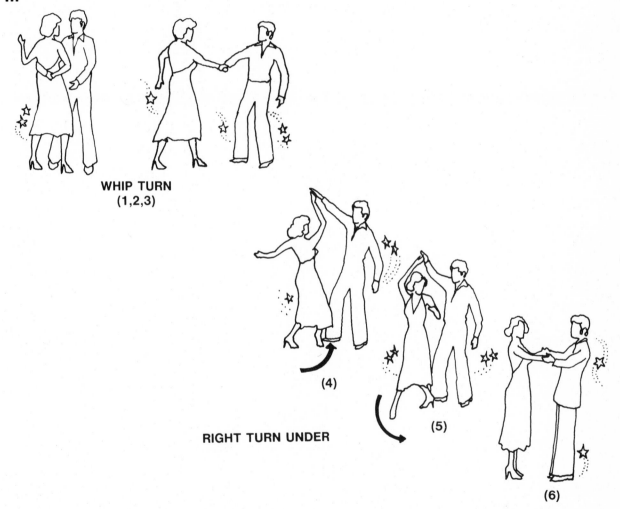

WHIP TURN
(1,2,3)

RIGHT TURN UNDER

(4)

(5)

(6)

IV REPEAT-SECTION II

STEP, BALL-CHANGE	STEP, BALL-CHANGE	DIP	STEP
(1, and -2)	(3, and -4)	(5)	(6)

DOUBLE STRUT

Double Strut. This is sort of a funky partner dance with 32 counts in four sections of eight counts each. The strut is a funky walk adopted by many of the best dancers. We call it the double strut here because it's really like taking two individuals doing a line dance and putting them together as partners. In other words, both partners do the steps with the same feet, rather than opposing feet as in most partner dances. This really is a good example of the fact that line dances can be adapted for couples. As such, the series below can also be done by an individual if you desire. Start in the swing position.

I. Start with a wrap turn right (1,2,3,4). Stay in the wrapped position and do a clockwise pinwheel turn (5,6,7,8). Note that you maintain this position while executing sections II and III.

II. This is where the double concept comes in. Both partners start with the right foot, as in a line dance, and do two jazz square walks (1,2,3,4,5,6,7,8).

III. The third section is also a double movement. Each partner does two kick-ball-

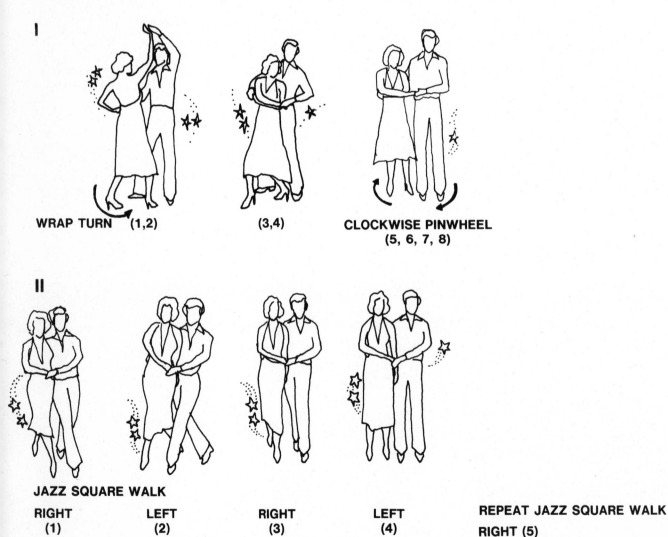

I

WRAP TURN (1,2)   (3,4)   CLOCKWISE PINWHEEL
(5, 6, 7, 8)

II

JAZZ SQUARE WALK

RIGHT   LEFT   RIGHT   LEFT   REPEAT JAZZ SQUARE WALK
(1)   (2)   (3)   (4)
                                                          RIGHT (5)
                                                          LEFT (6)
                                                          RIGHT (7)
                                                          LEFT (8)

changes, both starting with the right foot (1,and-2,3,and-4). Both partners then strut forward, stepping right, left, right, left (5,6,7,8).

IV.   To start the final section, the partners separate and each dancer does a three-point turn—the woman turning right, the man left—and holding open for the fourth count (1,2,3,4). To finish, the partners strut back to the beginning swing position (5,6,7,8).

For variety, try replacing the kick-ball-changes in Part III with two leg thrusts right, followed by two leg thrusts left.

III

KICK
(1)

BALL-CHANGE
(and 2)

REPEAT
KICK (3)
BALL-CHANGE (and 4)

STRUT FORWARD
STEP (5)
STEP (6)
STEP (7)
STEP (8)

IV

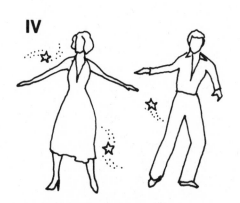

THREE POINT TURN
(1)

(2)

(3,4)

STRUT

STEP (5)
STEP (6)
STEP (7)
STEP (8)

DOUBLE STRUT

CHICAGO LOOP

CHICAGO LOOP

New Chicago Loop. Just as New York and Los Angeles have disco dance namesakes, Chicago dancers have developed their own favorites. The New Chicago Loop is a trendsetter in the Midwestern area and quite popular with our students. Based on an imitation of Chicago's downtown area, the Loop, it is a swirling, attractive dance using mainly circles in the form of loops, turns and rotations. The following series is in four sections of eight counts each—a total of 32 counts.

Keep in mind that in this dance, partners hands are clasped at all times except on the open break in Part III. Start in the swing position.

I. With the woman starting on the right foot and the man on the left, both partners touch side, step together, touch other side, step together (1,2,3,4). The next part of this section could be called a hip and arm loop. Each partner does a full hip rotation with knees close together, while looping the linked arms out to the sides, up and over the heads and back down to the middle, between partners (5,6,7,8).

II. The second section is a pinwheel lunge. Partners switch their position to the right straight arm pinwheel position and lunge forward once (1,2). Switch and lunge forward to the other side (3,4). Switch to the right-arm position again and do a complete pinwheel turn (5,6,7,8).

I

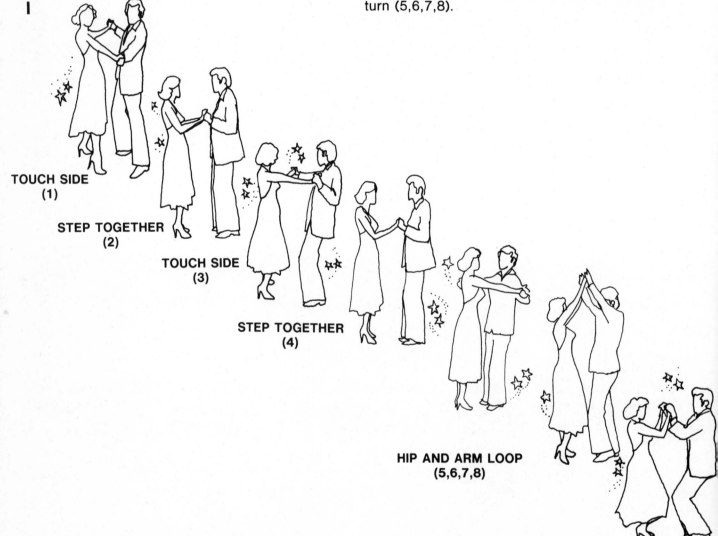

TOUCH SIDE
(1)

STEP TOGETHER
(2)

TOUCH SIDE
(3)

STEP TOGETHER
(4)

HIP AND ARM LOOP
(5,6,7,8)

III. The third section begins with another hip and arm loop (1,2,3,4). Then, do an open break (5,6), face each other again in the swing position (7) and both partners do a backward head drop (8).

IV. The fourth section is a grapevine loop. With the woman starting on the right foot and the man on the left, both partners do a grapevine to the same direction (1,2,3,4). Now repeat the grapevine in the opposite direction (5,6,7,8). The important part of this section is in the arms. As you execute the first grapevine, loop one set of linked arms by circling up over and through. When you change the direction of the grapevine, reverse the loop rotation of the arms.

II

PINWHEEL LUNGE

(1,2)   (3,4)   (5,6,7,8)

III

HIP AND ARM LOOP
(1,2,3,4)

OPEN BREAK
(5,6)

SWING POSITION
(7)

HEAD DROP
(8)

IV GRAPEVINE

SIDE
(1)

BACK
(2)

SIDE
(3)

TOGETHER
(4)

REPEAT GRAPEVINE (in opposite direction)

SIDE (5)
BACK (6)
SIDE (7)
TOGETHER (8)

By now you should be a confirmed discomaniac like the rest of us. If you followed instructions in this book carefully and practiced the exercises on a regular basis you should have enough knowledge to feel comfortable in any disco situation. Some of you may even want to go further and develop your skills to their fullest. Well, welcome to the club! Dance is the world's fastest growing art form and the best way we know to stay in shape.

Should you decide to expand on your training, be aware that *you do not have to sign a long-term contract* for a series of dance classes or practice sessions. What looks like a bargain deal can often leave you in a pinch. Nor is it necessary to invest in costly private lessons. Dancing is considered a group activity, so it is usually best to enroll in a group class. The constant source of energy which is emitted by a whirling group of dancers creates excitement and a good learning atmosphere. This does not mean the class should include 50 or 100 students crowded into one classroom or gymnasium. It would be very difficult to effect an individual teacher-pupil relationship in this kind of environment.

If you're looking for some really individualized disco moves, you might enjoy taking jazz dance classes at a professional dance studio. With the increased popularity of dance and a growing demand for instructors, self-made teachers are springing up everywhere. So be careful. Make sure the class members are in your own age group and ability level. Proper class placement is important, since some individuals become discouraged easily when trying to keep up with students who are obviously more advanced in their training. The experience of dancing with others of the same skill level often gives a new perspective on your own abilities and self-image.

As in any learning situation, you should seek out the most qualified teachers. The better the teacher, the greater his or her ability to demonstrate the steps and instill enthusiasm in the student. A school that produces eager, happy students does not need the insurance of contracts. An unqualified teacher, on the other hand, can completely destroy the self-confidence and mental outlook of a potentially good dancer by neglecting to break down various steps and combinations for the class. Watch out for teachers who talk a lot and teach little during class time. Their knowledge is usually as limited as yours. Almost as bad is the instructor who would rather put on a show for their captive audience than teach. There is no reason to waste your time and money on their ego trips.

Whatever your next goal, remember: you're already one step ahead just by owning this book. In doing so, you made the commitment to yourself that you are genuinely interested in disco dancing. The time and effort that you put into it depends on your desire and self-discipline, but it can add a new dimension to your life as it has for so many others.

The next chapter will introduce you to the disco scene and help round out your disco education. With this information, you will have everything you need to feel at home in the world of disco.

6
The
Disco Scene

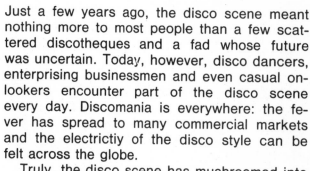

Just a few years ago, the disco scene meant nothing more to most people than a few scattered discotheques and a fad whose future was uncertain. Today, however, disco dancers, enterprising businessmen and even casual onlookers encounter part of the disco scene every day. Discomania is everywhere: the fever has spread to many commercial markets and the electrictiy of the disco style can be felt across the globe.

Truly, the disco scene has mushroomed into a worldwide subculture affecting the lives and lifestyles of millions. And it really is not surprising that this social phenomenon has spread so rapidly: the disco scene is based on a total immersion concept and citizens of every country are busily immersing themselves in the trappings of the craze.

The disco scene is made up of all the elements you would find in any discotheque, whether large or small, famous or obscure, super-flashy or modest. To set the stage for the disco scene, you must have a disco club with all its colors, lights and music; and disco people—dancers and otherwise—in all their glamorous finery. Again, you can find these ingredients just about anywhere you look today. But, to understand the inner workings of the disco world, you really have to step inside a discotheque and participate.

The Dance Emporium

For the enterprising businessman who loves the challenge of competition, the disco club is the modern alternative to the gold mine. As testament to the number of investors who have entered this market, discotheques open and close every day, with literally thousands in operation at any one time. For the investor who is willing to take the risk, opening a disco club can be quite profitable, but it does involve investing a small fortune.

To create the individual character that spells success for a particular club, the owner often must invest from $800,000 to $1,000,000, and sometimes even more. This expense goes toward hiring the services of renowned technical designers who come up with the special effects and total immersion themes that draw the disco crowds. To outfit a club like Studio 54, which incorporates 450 different special effects in all, that investment can be huge.

If the investor is lucky—and market-wise—his disco *will* attract dancers, and he can hope to stay in business for a couple of good years. Since the fickle public usually drifts from club to club, those first few years have to be good ones. For a popular club, cash turnover can reach an average of $16,000 a day—or night. With those receipts, it won't take long for an investor to recoup his starting costs. And expenses that continue during the club's operation are often lower than they would be for a nightclub or restaurant featuring live entertainment. The owner does not have to hire musicians, and this saving is in some cases passed on to his customers, who don't have to lay out lofty cover charges to pay for the band.

While disco—and the business it generates—is still growing by leaps and bounds, the potential earnings for a new disco club could decrease in the near future. Competition among discotheques has become so fervent that many clubs are bringing in live disco bands and disco dance shows to be featured in between dance sessions. Rivalry among owners has reached a peak, as one disco

Xenon, a New York City disco located near Times Square, opened one day and closed the next—only to reopen again some months later. (Wide World Photos)

Paramount Studios in Los Angeles was the scene for a huge disco party celebrating the premiere of Saturday Night Fever, *starring John Travolta and featuring music of the Bee Gees. (Wide World Photos)*

Can you identify this disco move? Steps, turns, and breaks soon become second nature to the accomplished disco dancer. (Courtesy Zorine's Disco)

Not all discos feature ultra-modern decor. Finley's in Chicago combines an antique motif with pulsating music. (Courtesy Finley's)

A sophisticated pinball machine invites dancers to a quiet corner of an antique-filled disco. (Courtesy The Rookery)

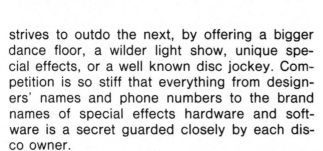

Signs of the times

strives to outdo the next, by offering a bigger dance floor, a wilder light show, unique special effects, or a well known disc jockey. Competition is so stiff that everything from designers' names and phone numbers to the brand names of special effects hardware and software is a secret guarded closely by each disco owner.

In response to what seems an infinite demand for new discotheques, clubs have popped up in suburbs and rural areas, which may be the new target for the disco investor. In large cities such as New York and Los Angeles, only the best clubs survive, indicating possible failure for the hapless owner who invests in costly accoutrements that just don't measure up in the eyes of the dancers. But in rural areas and suburbs the selection and variety of clubs is not as broad, making the public less likely to seek greener disco pastures. So

the clever investor may actually do better to find a small town that hankers for a disco club and probably will be loyal to it.

Besides the whole spectrum of disco clubs found in the cities, dancers now can disco just about anywhere they can walk. Disco franchises are the biggest new entry into the discotheque world. Soon Americans will be able to patronize their favorite disco no matter which city they visit, making the sight of the 2001 and Tramps franchises as common as were the Arthur Murray dance studios during the '50s.

Another new home for the disco club is the major hotel chains. Hilton Hotels now feature discos in some locations, and Billboard's Disco Forum IV was held in the New York Hilton in 1978. Some health spa chains also are adding discos to their facilities, and several well traveled, resort-area airports may soon offer discos to those passing through. Finally, some department store basements now offer disco rooms meant to attract female patrons.

No matter where the club, most of the investor's initial outlay goes toward creating a total atmosphere of glamor and fantasy. The principal aim of most discos is to make everyone feel like a star, and the first step to accomplishing this is setting the stage fully. Thanks to modern technology, the disco has reached new heights in technical design. Many clubs combine the campy glamor of Art Deco interiors with the futuristic effects of laser beams and fifty to a hundred sound speakers.

In general, the disco club has a huge and often underlit dance floor which is the focal point of the discotheque. The idea, after all, is to draw dancers onto the floor. The other components of the club are designed around a particular theme to come up with the total immersion concept in atmospheres. We've seen disco clubs in the U.S. and elsewhere which have used designs ranging from chrome-and-white modern to elegant Victorian to balloon-and-streamer sock hop—each somehow evoking an ever-current disco look.

The hypnotic designs often feature mirrored balls or multifaceted prisms that spin above the dancers, casting ever-changing reflections and colors throughout the room. The Plexiglas or stainless steel dance floors flash with colored lights that change with the tempo and intensity of the music. Feathers and ivory can be juxtaposed against the gleaming silver of a science fiction space vehicle, or W. C. Fields movies are projected onto wall screens above plush velvet banquettes. Uniqueness is the characteristic that every owner seeks in his club. And, like the primitive tribal rituals of a lost age, each disco strives to stimulate and energize all the senses of the dancers.

To increase the intricacy of the disco's effects, many owners use several levels, or series of balconies and staircases. The more there is for the patron to explore, the less likely that he or she will become bored with the club. Dillon's, a popular Los Angeles club, actually has four separate floors. Only one floor has loud music and a dance floor; the others are quiet enough for conversation but provide closed-circuit television views of the action on other levels.

This actually has become one of the latest

Disco dance floors are frequently lighted from below. This sequence, shot in Chicago's Galaxy, shows the changing patterns of light that help bring magic to dancers' feet. (Courtesy The Galaxy)

trends in disco clubs. In an attempt to draw additional patrons, many clubs feature activities besides dancing. Many discos combine dancing and dining. Other clubs are restaurants until 9 p.m. or later, when disco takes over. Or, a disco may have a dining area sectioned off from the rest of the club, with a wall that can be opened for the disco patrons. The Las Vegas Hilton actually turns its buffet luncheon room into a disco at night, merely by lowering a hydraulic stage to make a separate dance floor. Many discos also incorporate bars, lounges and game rooms filled with pinball machines, electronic games and backgammon tables, pool and billiard tables.

In New York and elsewhere, Studio 54 is one of the most famous discos ever to open. Its original 450 special effects included a fog and perfume machine, red smoke that puffs up from the dance floor, fake snowfalls and a

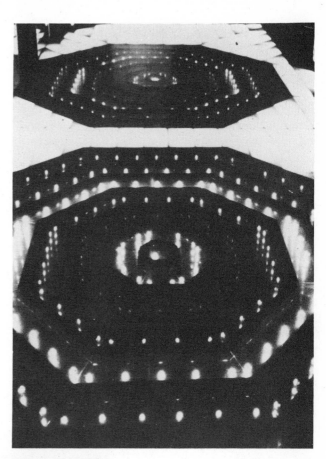

Studio 54 in New York City is a trendsetter in disco decor. (Globe Photos)

giant half moon that lowers from the ceiling with a glowing nose and a small spoon. But Studio 54, which takes its name from the CBS studio it once was, takes greater pride in the most special of all its effects—its clientele. Studio 54 takes exclusivity to the extreme, admitting a carefully scrutinized and hand-picked few from the scores of would-be dancers that often stand outside.

Exclusivity is not limited to Studio 54, however. Many clubs have members-only policies, with average initiation fees ranging from $25 to $1,000; some require monthly dues as well. The trick in these policies is to know how far to go, of course. Some clubs have either failed or revamped their policies after driving patrons away with excessive restrictions on who gets in and who stays out.

Some clubs try to achieve the client mix they want by establishing a dress code. Often, the dress code is unwritten, so consult someone who has been there before you waltz into a new disco in bluejeans.

Besides the quantity and quality of speakers used in the well equipped disco, a plethora of other sound-control devices has been produced in response to disco needs. Computerized turn tables and huge record libraries can be found at the disc jockey's side, and expensive mixers, preamplifiers and other components are constantly added. Decibel meters are now becoming a common tool in discos, since experts suspect that DJs and other employees of discos have suffered loss of hearing from the music's volume.

Resident disc jockeys select music, control pace and volume, often direct light shows, and frequently run dance contests. Disc jockeys in important discos yield a significant force in determining sales for disco records. (Courtesy The Galaxy)

But even with all the right ingredients, the recipe for the successful disco can be tough to follow. In some cases, the new owner can end up with a multi-million-dollar spectacular failure. To start off well and stay in business, many club owners depend on constant publicity, which they usually receive from a willing, if sometimes critical, press.

In one spectacular opening, 2,500 guests poured through the doors of a new Big Apple disco called Xenon, or *stranger*. Patrons ranged from Hollywood and Broadway celebrities to anonymous dancers with silver spray-painted bodies, mirrored and gold mesh costumes and exhibiting every dance style known. Unfortunately, Xenon was apparently not quite ready to open. Many of the lights didn't work and some walls were not yet painted; the design's highlight, a giant spaceship that was to lower from the ceiling, was deemed unimpressive because its lights also failed to operate. And the general crowd opinion was that the dance floor wasn't more than half the size of that of Studio 54. Xenon closed after opening night, to reopen sometime later.

Besides making you feel like a star, and surrounding you with disco atmosphere, the goal of most clubs is to invite you to entertain yourself. Unlike the nightclubs and cabarets of the past, in which patrons paid to be entertained by live music, comedy and dance, the disco says to its patrons: It's party time and everyone's invited. In many cases, young people have deserted the singles bars in favor of discos, some of which do not even serve liquor. Most clubs offer a mixture of singles and couples, so regardless of marital status, you have a chance to meet people and to dance. Some couples, who met at a particular disco, have been known to hold their marriage ceremonies at that club.

The highlight of participation in the disco is the dance contest. Held weekly in many clubs, the contests are usually run by the resident DJ, and offer monetary prizes and trophies to the best dancers. Three types of contest usually are included in the events. The Anything Goes contest is just that; couples, singles doing freestyle, and groups doing line dances can enter. The Couples Only event is usually quite popular with those who have practiced routines with regular partners, but to make sure the odds are not stacked against single dancers who are skilled at partner dances as well, many clubs include a Jack and Jill contest. In this event, the contestants' names are thrown into two hats for male and female dancers and partners are matched at random.

Probably the most spectacular tribute to the world of disco is *Billboard's* Disco Forum. Originally held annually, the event has become so important that in 1978 it became a semiannual jamboree. Disco Forum IV, held in June of 1978 at the New York Hilton, honored disco pioneers and veterans alike, giving awards for the most promising new disco artist of the year—Linda Clifford—and overall disco artist of the year—Donna Summer. Cerrone was honored with five separate awards (see chapter 2), and Casablanca, which has produced some of the biggest disco records and films, was named disco record label of the year. The forum also gave awards for best disco promotion people, best club consultant, best franchiser, best new audio product and best new lighting product. The DJs, of course, received special attention, with disc jockey regional awards going to 16 notables.

The Disco Costume

The clothes worn by disco patrons are as much a part of the atmosphere as the dance floor and the colored lights. Watching the dressed-up crowds outside of Studio 54 is like seeing one big casting call for a one-night show. Again, the idea is to be noticed, to be a star. In most cases, the only rule is to let your imagination run wild in adorning yourself for a disco night. If you wear a nurse's uniform during the day, you can disco at night dressed as Cleopatra. If you carry a postal bag full of mail during the afternoon, you can don skin-tight slacks and a silky shirt to turn you into a Valentino of the '70s for the evening. No one really cares who you are; what you wear and how you dance speak for themselves.

If you have no idea of what to wear at a disco club, try following some of these tips. First and foremost is comfort. If your clothing is binding, your evening can be ruined. Generally, one of the best costumes for a woman is a full, swirling skirt and a somewhat bare top. The wide skirts look gorgeous when you twirl around the dance floor and give you plenty of mobility. Halter, strapless or just plain sleeve-less tops are really helpful when you build up a fever on the floor. Whatever you wear, it should be comfortable and cool.

For men, the standard outfit of today seems to be extra-slim trousers and a shimmering, colorful shirt. Dancers can add matching vests or jackets at their will. Whether you are male or female, of course, there are many diversions from this average costume. Wherever the club, check dress codes ahead of your visit. In some places, blue jeans and t-shirts may still be acceptable, but the trend is much more elegant or formal in most clubs. Discos have also affected the clothing industry. The lightweight skirt-and-top outfits so popular with female dancers can be found in just about any metropolitan department store. And designers like Halston are now creating and marketing clothing intended specifically for disco dancing.

Clothing and dance styles are quite different according to the region—or nation—that you disco in. On the East Coast, and especially in New York, which probably is the disco captial of the world, dancing is sophisticated but outrageous as are the clothes the dancers wear. "Anything goes" is the motto of the dancers, and new styles are often born in this region.

On the West Coast, clothing and dance styles run toward the freewheeling. Freestyle dance is stressed, as are lock dances, for which dancers wear a punk style costume (see L.A. Lock, Chapter 5). It's not the safety-pin-and-rags punk style of New York and London punk rock, but the look is just as identifiable and is often called funky or punk.

The Midwest, as always, is in the middle of things, incorporating some of each coast's dress styles, plus some intricate partner stylings of its own.

The Dancers

If you don't believe at this point that anyone can enter the world of disco, there's nothing more we can say. The only thing that will prove it to you is a firsthand look at the inside of a discotheque.

Originating with the younger set, disco is now an activity pursued by dancers of all ages. With the game rooms and lounges that many clubs feature, there really is something for everyone, even if you don't intend to dance the night away. And with the complex combination of influences from different decades, disco fans from age six to 60 can find something familiar and alluring. Older dancers often hit the discos because they like the idea of returning to the custom of frequent social dancing. Some older dancers feel there's nothing to make you feel young again like disco dancing. Younger dancers, on the other hand, are caught up in this fast-paced trend and have the energy to stay on the dance floor for hours. Many regular disco dancers are night people who work during the afternoon or evening and stay out till dawn at the discos. It has even become a custom in some clubs to gather a die-hard group at closing time to go out for breakfast—or head for an after-hours discotheque.

This type of lifestyle is led by many disc jockeys as well. While many DJs, as well as waitresses and other disco employees, hold day jobs, they take their disco work quite seriously. Regulars at discos who have become accomplished dancers often have been offered jobs as dance teachers. Some even forsake their daytime employment for the glamor and fun of a disco-oriented job. Among them are those who have opened their own disco catering services. For a certain fee, the service brings light shows, sound equipment, dancers for instruction or a show, and a disc jockey right into your home to turn your living room into the ultimate in exclusive discotheques.

Getting the message? Everyone is doing it. Why not join the fun?

INDEX OF DISCO DANCES

INDEX OF STEPS, TURNS AND BREAKS

SUBJECT INDEX